HELP!
I'm Bored in Church

Entering fully into worship in the Divine Liturgy

David Smith

ANCIENT FAITH
PUBLISHING

The Ancient Christian Faith for the Modern World

Chesterton, Indiana

Help! I'm Bored in Church
Entering fully into worship in the Divine Liturgy

Scripture quotations are taken from the New King James Version,
© 1979, 1980, 1982 by Thomas Nelson, Inc. Used by permission.

Published by   Ancient Faith Publishing
                    (formerly known as Conciliar Press)
                    A division of Ancient Faith Ministries
                    P.O. Box 748
                    Chesterton, IN 46304

Printed in the United States of America

ISBN 10: 1-936270-64-1

ISBN 13: 978-1-936270-64-4

Contents

Chapter One

What Is Boredom?

My original title for this book was *Church Is Boring.*

You might react to that title by saying, *Of course it's boring. Finally you're admitting it.* If even priests admit that church is boring, then that settles it. We can all stay home and sleep in on Sundays.

Or perhaps you think it's irreverent to say, "Church is boring." You're thinking, *It's not right for you to speak about the Divine Liturgy like that. If the priest says church is boring, he shouldn't be a priest.* You don't find church boring, and your only complaint is that it's not longer.

Or it's more likely that you're in the middle. Church seems boring at times, yes. But there's something good about church as well, and so saying "church is boring" makes you a little uncomfortable. You're probably going to go to church for the rest of your life; at least there's no reason you wouldn't. So if you admit that it's boring, won't you just make yourself unhappy? Church is not going to change, so is it really helpful to admit that it's sometimes a little bit of a grind to get through it? On certain feast days, or on a Sunday when the priest goes on and on with an incomprehensible sermon, or when the choir or the chanters seem to be singing the song that never ends, badly—what's going on in your mind? If you admit you're bored, won't that make you stop wanting to go to church?

No, it won't. It won't because the fact that you're sometimes bored says something about you, not about the Church. And you can change you. You can't make the Divine Liturgy any shorter, but you can accomplish something within yourself that makes the time you spend in the Liturgy an experience of spiritual delight. Useful. Necessary. Something you look forward to.

My purpose is to invite you to enter completely into the worship of the Orthodox Church. You may go to church every Sunday, or occasionally, or perhaps not at all. It doesn't matter, because all of us need to respond to the invitation to experience the fullness, the beauty, the holiness of Orthodox worship. If you don't, you might attend Divine Liturgy off and on for the rest of your life, but there will be times, perhaps many times—perhaps many times during each Liturgy—when you'll be bored.

No, the Church is not going to change. My question is this: How can *you* change, how can *I* change, so that each moment of each Divine Liturgy— and each moment of the prayers, the sacraments, the vespers and vigils—lifts us into the heavenly kingdom, just like the prophet Isaiah when he had his vision:

> In the year that King Uzziah died, I saw the Lord sitting on a throne, high and lifted up, and the train of His *robe* filled the temple. Above it stood seraphim; each one had six wings: with two he covered his face, with two he covered his feet, and with two he flew. And one cried to another and said: "Holy, holy, holy is the LORD of hosts; the whole earth *is* full of His glory!" (Is. 6:1–3)

We're not going to use our imaginations, and we're not going to stir up our emotions in order to make this happen. No, those are dead ends. Many have tried those methods, and many are trying them still. They are exhausting and pointless. But what other options do we have? How does one enter into the worship of the Church in a meaningful, mature, spiritual manner?

Let's start by defining the word *boredom*.

Imagine you're holding a thousand dollars in your hand, and as you watch, it dissolves into nothing. You do what you can to stop this from happening, but the bill just keeps dissolving until it's all gone. That's a picture of boredom. You have something—in this case time, not money—that you want to spend on things you like or need. But the time dissolves into nothing before your eyes, and no matter what you do, you can't stop it from happening. So here's a definition of boredom: It's the feeling you get when your time is dissolving into nothing and you can't stop it from happening.

One part of my definition is very important for our discussion: Boredom is a *feeling*. It's emotional. Boredom is not the thousand dollars dissolving away. Boredom is the anger and helplessness and frustration and sadness you feel while it's dissolving. It's a horrible feeling. But it is a feeling. *Boredom* does not describe being trapped; it describes the feeling you get when you think you're trapped. Boredom is not wasted time; it's the feeling you get when you decide your time is being wasted.

Are there some things that are just plain boring, in and of themselves? I don't think so. For instance, I find NASCAR races boring. But I know people who love them, who work all week long at their jobs in order to sit and watch a race on the weekend. They talk about it and learn about it and predict what will happen and just love it. I can't. I don't get it. On the other hand, I like hockey. I love watching my favorite NHL team. And guess what? I have close friends who have tried to watch hockey with me and find it terrifically boring.

So, tell me—is NASCAR boring? Is hockey boring? Or football, or mountain climbing, or gourmet cooking, or watching TV, or shopping, or going to concerts? To some people, yes, one or more of these things is boring.

But no one activity is boring to everyone in the world. Boredom is not a characteristic of any particular activity or pastime. Boredom is inside you.

Where does church appear on that list? Some find services boring, and others wish they were longer. But we can say one thing for sure: It has nothing to do with church. It has to do with our emotions. The word *boredom* describes the feelings we have when we think we're trapped or our time is being wasted. No one is trapped in the Church, but sometimes you *feel* trapped.

Many of us have had the feeling at one point or another that church felt a little like a waste of time, like there were better things we could have been doing. We have to make two specific steps before we can feel that way. The first is when our minds wander off to another place, and the second is when our minds say, *Hey, I'd rather be there than here.* That's when we start to feel bored. Most of what we'll be talking about in this book is how to keep our minds from wandering around like a kid lost in a mall.

You also feel bored when you feel like you're not being challenged. That happens when the task before you is too simple. If I'm sitting in a class, and the teacher is droning on and on about something I don't understand, I'm bored because I've given up on the lesson. In this case, I've dismissed myself from the challenge of understanding what he's talking about and have given myself a new challenge: trying to stay awake until it's over. That's a fairly simple task. And a boring one. Likewise, if I'm in a class and the teacher is droning on and on about something I already understand, then I'm bored for a different reason, but the result is the same. I sit there, just waiting for it to end.

We are going to find a challenge in church that will keep us from ever saying, "My goal is to just sit (or stand) here until this ends."

There are times in our lives when all of us have to learn to deal with boredom at some job we have. I know someone who is a great example. Her job is to open letters all day. That's all she does. She works for an insurance company, and for eight hours every day, she opens their mail. That's boring, to be sure. She has every right to feel both trapped and unchallenged.

Here's the thing, though. She keeps going to work every day. She has told me she will keep that job till retirement, if they let her stay that long. How can a person do something as boring as open letters all day? First, she's there for the money, not the excitement. Also, she has other challenges that give her life meaning. Third, she listens to music or audiobooks on her iPod all day, and that's where she puts her mind. Put these three things together, and you have someone who is doing a numbingly boring job, but who is not bored. She understands that boredom is an emotion, and she is not going to allow her life to be dictated by emotions. She has addressed the monotony of her job head on and found ways to avoid the emotional drain of boredom. That's a smart woman.

So what about you? Look at it this way: If you feel cold, you put on a coat. If you feel hungry, you eat. What do you do if you feel bored? I'll tell you, you need to do *something*. It's a sad and pathetic person who is cold and says, *I'm cold but I don't care enough about myself to put on a coat. I'll just suffer and be unhappy.* Would you do that? Certainly not! Well, don't do it when you're bored in church either. This is your challenge: Discover the coat you need to put on, and then—put it on!

I'll give you the answer that has worked for me: The coat consists of prayer and watchfulness. No, it doesn't sound easy and it doesn't sound fun. Because it's not. Prayer is something that all of us do now and then, some more than others. But we can never do watchfulness "now and then." Watchfulness is difficult because we need to train ourselves to practice it constantly. It's a skill we develop throughout our lives.

But now we have another problem. I've told you where we're going, and I've revealed to you that the challenge is not an easy one. Here's a good question: Why do it? Why go to church at all? If going to church requires a skill that takes a lot of effort to develop, why make that effort? Does the advantage really outweigh the price?

Let's go back to my illustration. The fact that my friend who works at the insurance company gets paid to be there makes her situation very different from your attendance at church. Her compelling and primary reason to go to work is that they pay her. If they didn't pay her at the insurance company, she would have to go and find a job somewhere else. She would not simply stay home like someone skipping church. She could stay home and fight boredom by listening to her iPod—but she wouldn't. She would be out looking for a job. For an income—for money.

So let me ask you: Where is the "money" in your attendance at the Divine Liturgy? What do you get from going to church? That's an important question. If you feel like you're not getting anything from church, you're not going to consider going there very important. You'll address boredom by simply not going. So we'll start with that question, and answer it four different ways.

(1) At church you get atonement.

We start with the atonement because when we decide what we believe about the atonement, we gain the foundation upon which we build our faith. I define *atonement* as that part of our faith that tells us *how* we have fellowship with God. It answers questions like these: What do I gain from the various elements of our faith? What has God done, and what do I do, in order that we might live in harmony with each other? Why does our worship look the way it does, and how does it give me access to God? These are critical questions, and if you can answer them, you've gone a good way toward understanding why you go to church in the first place. And why it's worth your effort to address the problem of boredom.

And, oh, by the way, we'll learn about the atonement using pictures. Word pictures. If you're like me, you understand theology better if it has pictures.

(2) At church you get the Divine Liturgy.

Next we discuss the Divine Liturgy. Here's what some people say: "Hey, if church is boring, let's change the Liturgy and make it shorter and more interesting." Perhaps even you've said that, if only to yourself. So, why not? If we don't ask, we'll never know.

(3) At church you get more than you bargain for.

Third, I want to look at the visible versus the invisible Liturgy. A priest wrote an article about people in his parish who never came to church, but instead watched the Liturgy on TV from the old country. They told him they wanted to see "the splendid vestments of the bishops and priests and . . . [hear] the beautiful voices of the deacons as they chant the petitions in Greek." One of the men said to him, "The authentic and splendid Byzantine iconography and those chanters remind me of my old village in Greece. Every Saturday we can relive the glories of Byzantium and the cultural heritage of our people."[1]

Contrast this with going to a church where you can't even hear the priest or understand him. The choir is terrible and the icons are amateurish. The vestments are old, and besides, they're always asking for money. And along

---

1   Fr. John S. Bakas, "Cultural Televangelism," *Orthodox Observer*, February–March 2012, p. 9.

with that, you have to sit on a wooden bench rather than on your couch or easy chair at home.

What's so glorious and heavenly about the Divine Liturgy? It sometimes doesn't look that great at all. Do I actually have to go to the church itself and sit through the service?

(4) At church you can eat the flesh of God.

Finally, it comes down to this: The church is the only place where you can get the bread that is sent from heaven, the Body and Blood of Christ. In the Divine Liturgy, we eat the flesh of God and drink His blood. There is no other place on earth where you can do that or anything even close to that. Can you imagine anyone saying they have the Body and Blood of God, and they're going to offer it to you to eat and drink? Anyone besides the Church would have to be insane to say something like that. In chapter five we're going to look at a time in our Lord's life when He told people about Holy Communion, and almost all of them stopped following Him because they thought His words were crazy and disgusting.

THAT'S THE MONEY. My four reasons—"Why go at all?"—give you a purpose for going to church. Then, after that, we can look at the occasional feelings of boredom. Remember? If you're cold, you put on a coat. If you're bored, you put on prayer and watchfulness.

After we look at the reasons we get bored in church, and some ideas of what you might do right in the Divine Liturgy to address this problem, we'll spend our last chapters rising a little higher. You're not a child. Sure, church is boring sometimes, but a mature person learns—more than learns, in fact, struggles—to make the time real, valuable, and life-giving.

Think of someone like St. Seraphim of Sarov. He spent years sitting in a little hut in the forest. What would that be like? I think after a few days I would wish for a visitor or two to speak with, but when visitors came to see St. Seraphim, he hid in a hole under the floor of his hut until his visitors went away. What was he doing all that time he lived alone in the forest? He was waiting. Waiting on God, which is the best use of time this world has to offer.

Of course, he was waiting on God by praying. We're going to look at the two parts of us that pray, and the two kinds of prayer: private and public. When you're in church, you're participating in public prayer. But you can carry private prayer with you into the church; that's the kind of prayer St. Seraphim was doing. You can't get much more private than he was. Private prayer is the prayer you do when you're alone. Yes, there are times when you're attending some kind of public prayer and it drags a little bit. But private prayer never drags; in fact, time stops altogether when you learn to pray the prayer of the heart. Sometimes it's good to have private prayer with you when you're in church and you're getting distracted.

But of course, you need to practice private prayer for it to work. Having private prayer with you as a kind of backup when you go to church won't work if you never pray privately. Imagine you're at a boring lecture in school or at a pointless meeting at work, and you have a video game or a phone or something in your pocket that would help pass the time. When you try to sneak it out of your pocket to use it, you discover it's not charged. Whatever you've got in your hand isn't going to help at all! Same with prayer. You definitely have to charge your private prayer in order for it to work when you need it. The thing that charges your private prayer is silence.

That's the one thing you need. More than electricity, more than a bathroom, more than heat or air conditioning, more than food. You need silence.

Some of you have been so starved for silence, you can't even remember that you need it.

So are you ready? Let's say it out loud: "Sometimes church is boring." Okay. Good. Now let's do something about it.

Part I

Why Go at All?

Chapter Two

Atonement

SOME YEARS AGO I was speaking with a young man who had dropped out of high school. He had not gone to school for almost a year when I met him, and when I started to talk to him about going back, he made it clear he would not do that. He was tall and good-looking. He wasn't smart, but he was enthusiastic and fun to be with.

Imagine yourself standing in front of that young man, trying to persuade him to go back to school. What would you say? *Shouldn't you think about the future?* He didn't want to. *What are you doing with your time, anyway?* He didn't know. Hanging out. *School's not so bad—get some help.* He said he didn't need any help, he just wasn't going to school. How about, *Your friends are in school, aren't they? You want to be where they are, I'm sure.* No. Most of his friends were doing exactly what he was doing. Nothing.

This young man was in a homeless shelter where I was working, and I tried everything to get him to take a look at his future. Nothing seemed to work. He was convinced that anyone who kept going to school after they were legally able to withdraw was a fool.

How about you? Did you continue to go to school after you turned sixteen? Probably you did, or if you're not yet sixteen, certainly you will. Tell me—do you feel like a fool? Of course not. You would have felt like a fool if you had *stopped* going to school. Let's think about this for a moment. This young man says only fools go to school. Some people agree with him, but others feel just the opposite. How does this happen? What could possibly lead people to such different conclusions?

I have an idea. I really think the young man I was speaking to did not clearly understand the *purpose* for going to school in the first place. That was his problem. Someone had said to him, "School is useless" or something like that, and he believed them. Thus, he had only one purpose in going to school: to keep out of juvenile detention. Then when he turned sixteen he was home free.

If you don't understand the purpose for something, you might put up with it for awhile, but ultimately you get bored. After you decide you're wasting your time, all you want to do is get out. On the other hand, when you have purpose, you can face the most difficult challenges imaginable. Toward the end of my seminary studies, I served as the youth pastor in a church, held two jobs, and carried eighteen graduate credit hours. I used to say to my wife, "I'll sleep when I graduate." How could I have possibly done all that? I wanted to graduate from seminary. I wanted to be ordained. I wanted to do what I'm doing right now, and I was determined nothing would stop me. I had a purpose, and my purpose gave me resolve. Coffee helped, but my sense of purpose was stronger.

This is what I want you to have in relation to going to church. If you understand why you're in church, then being there for a long time, or being there every Sunday, will not get in your way of enjoying the worship of Almighty God. We need resolve. And purpose. And we're going to get it first by looking at the basic elements of God's relationship with mankind, which we call the atonement.

The Atonement: It's a Marriage

Picture yourself in the perfect marriage. What words would you use to describe how great that is? Every possible way you can describe the perfect marriage accurately describes your relationship to God—or rather, your soul's marriage to God.

- **Peace:** "These things I have spoken to you, that in Me you may have peace. In the world you will have tribulation; but be of good cheer, I have overcome the world." (John 16:33)

- **Sharing everything:** "In that day you will ask Me nothing. Most assuredly, I say to you, whatever you ask the Father in My name He will give you. . . . Ask, and you will receive, that your joy may be full." (John 16:23–24)

- **Mutual support:** "Most assuredly, I say to you, he who believes in Me, the works that I do he will do also; and greater *works* than these he will do, because I go to My Father." (John 14:12)

- **Physical intimacy:**

    "Come, my beloved,

    Let us go forth to the field;

    Let us lodge in the villages.

    Let us get up early to the vineyards;

    Let us see if the vine has budded,

    Whether the grape blossoms are open,

    And the pomegranates are in bloom.

    There I will give you my love.

    The mandrakes give off a fragrance,

    And at our gates *are* pleasant *fruits*,

    All manner, new and old,

    Which I have laid up for you, my beloved." (Song 7:11–13)

and:

> "When He had given thanks, He broke *it* and said, 'Take, eat; this is
> My body which is broken for you; do this in remembrance of Me.'
> In the same manner *He* also *took* the cup after supper, saying, 'This
> cup is the new covenant in My blood. This do, as often as you drink
> *it*, in remembrance of Me.'" (1 Cor. 11:23–26)

- **Building a beautiful family:** "Therefore if *there* is any consolation in
  Christ, if any comfort of love, if any fellowship of the Spirit, if any affec-
  tion and mercy, fulfill my joy by being like-minded, having the same
  love, *being* of one accord, of one mind. *Let* nothing *be done* through selfish ambition or conceit, but in lowliness of mind let each esteem others
  better than himself. Let each of you look out not only for his own interests, but also for the interests of others." (Phil. 2:1–4)

- **Stability:** "And I give them eternal life, and they shall never perish; neither shall anyone snatch them out of My hand." (John 10:28)

- **Joy:** "Though now you do not see *Him*, yet believing, you rejoice with
  joy inexpressible and full of glory, receiving the end of your faith—the
  salvation of *your* souls" (1 Peter 1:8–9).

Try to think of some other words that would describe a perfect marriage.
They all pertain to the soul's relationship to God, don't they?

But there's a problem. There's another "lover." Not God's, but yours:
"For I have betrothed you to one husband, that I may present *you as* a chaste
virgin to Christ. But I fear, lest somehow, as the serpent deceived Eve by
his craftiness, so your minds may be corrupted from the simplicity that is in
Christ" (2 Cor. 11:2–3). For some reason, and you can't imagine why, you
find yourself leaving your beautiful home and marriage and running to meet
one with whom you commit adultery: "And supper being ended, the devil

having already put it into the heart of Judas Iscariot, Simon's *son*, to betray Him" (John 13:2).

Even as you drive to the tryst you scold yourself for doing it, but you keep driving. And when you arrive, you fall into the arms of the other one, the cheat and liar, the destroyer: "The field is the world, the good seeds are the sons of the kingdom, but the tares are the sons of the wicked *one*. The enemy who sowed them is the devil" (Matt. 13:38–39). You hate it there, but you find it almost impossible to stay away.

The adulterer does not love you; he hates you, in fact: "Woe to the inhabitants of the earth and the sea! For the devil has come down to you, having great wrath, because he knows that he has a short time" (Rev. 12:12b).

Sometimes you make plans to meet and he doesn't come. When you call to find out why, he laughs and hangs up: "Be sober, be vigilant; because your adversary the devil walks about like a roaring lion, seeking whom he may devour" (1 Peter 5:8).

He lies to you constantly: "Then the serpent said to the woman, 'You will not surely die'" (Gen. 3:4). "You are of *your* father the devil, and the desires of your father you want to do. He was a murderer from the beginning, and does not stand in the truth, because there is no truth in him. When he speaks a lie, he speaks from his own *resources*, for he is a liar and the father of it" (John 8:44).

If you try to say anything, he tells you to shut up. There is no peace, no sharing, no support, no family, and no joy:

"For the lips of an immoral woman drip honey,

And her mouth is smoother than oil;

But in the end she is bitter as wormwood,

Sharp as a two-edged sword" (Prov. 5:3–4)

All he wants from you is that you leave your marriage and join him: "Those by the wayside are the ones who hear; then the devil comes and takes away the word out of their hearts, lest they should believe and be saved" (Luke 8:12).

Again, this describes the relationship of the soul, but not with God.

Your soul has the opportunity for something better than the most perfect relationship human minds can imagine: "Eye has not seen, nor ear heard, / Nor have entered into the heart of man / The things which God has prepared for those who love Him" (1 Cor. 2:9).

And yet you constantly turn away from it: "For the good that I will *to do*, I do not do; but the evil I will not *to do*, that I practice. Now if I do what I will not *to do*, it is no longer I who do it, but sin that dwells in me. I find then a law, that evil is present with me, the one who wills to do good. For I delight in the law of God according to the inward man. But I see another law in my members, warring against the law of my mind, and bringing me into captivity to the law of sin which is in my members. O wretched man that I am! Who will deliver me from this body of death?" (Rom. 7:19–24).

How can this be? How can you have the best possible life available right in front of you and decide to walk away from it? And we all do it. Constantly! I don't have an answer for that one.

While you are spending time with the devil in his crummy hotel room, you hear someone knocking at the door: "Behold, I stand at the door and knock. If anyone hears My voice and opens the door, I will come in to him and dine with him, and he with Me" (Rev. 3:20).

You open the door and find Jesus standing there. He's come to that part of the city, to that hotel, up the filthy steps, along the hall reeking with the odors of human waste: "For Christ also suffered once for sins, the just for the unjust, that He might bring us to God, being put to death in the flesh but made alive by the Spirit, by whom also He went and preached to the spirits in prison" (1 Pet. 3:18–19).

He has found the room where you are and has come to rescue you: "But you *are* a chosen generation, a royal priesthood, a holy nation, His own special people, that you may proclaim the praises of Him who called you out of darkness into His marvelous light" (1 Pet. 2:9).

When you open the door and look into His eyes, you know immediately what you should do: "*that* they may come to their senses *and escape* the snare of the devil, having been taken captive by him to *do* his will" (2 Tim. 2:26).

You step into the hall: "Then I heard a loud voice saying in heaven, 'Now salvation, and strength, and the kingdom of our God, and the power of His Christ have come, for the accuser of our brethren, who accused them before our God day and night, has been cast down'" (Rev. 12:10).

He puts His arm around your shoulder, and the two of you make your way back home: "Therefore submit to God. Resist the devil and he will flee from you" (James 4:7).

God is waiting. He runs out of the house into the driveway when you and your Savior drive up, and embraces you as you emerge from the car: "And he arose and came to his father. But when he was still a great way off, his father saw him and had compassion, and ran and fell on his neck and kissed him" (Luke 15:20).

He brings you back inside the house, tends to the wounds you received from the devil, and the beautiful marriage you had before is restored: "If we confess our sins, He is faithful and just to forgive us *our* sins and to cleanse us from all unrighteousness" (1 John 1:9).

Fr. John Romanides wrote: "The purpose of the communion of the life-giving flesh of Christ through the Spirit is to cast out the powers of sins that reign through death and corruptibility, to restore the source of immortality to man, and to return man to the way of perfection and theosis."[2] And later, in the same work, "God showed mercy to the one who had been deceived."[3]

This is how I want you to think about your relationship to God—like a marriage. A perfect marriage—except that you commit adultery nearly every day. But here's the good news: God will always welcome you back. He will always run out to the car to hug you and walk with you back into your home. *But you have to go home.* You can't sit in the hotel with the devil, leave Christ knocking at the door, and think you can make your relationship right with God. How are you going to do that? Over the phone? Text him? No, not at all. You've got to leave the destroyer and go back to the Life-giver.

Now I want you to notice something. What is the first thing you do when you go back into the house you and God share? You're going to repent:

"How I have hated instruction,

And my heart despised correction!

I have not obeyed the voice of my teachers,

Nor inclined my ear to those who instructed me!

I was on the verge of total ruin,

In the midst of the assembly and congregation" (Proverbs 5:12–14)

Confession is the front door. You have to talk about what you've done. When I meet with couples who are trying to work through adultery, I'm amazed at how often the injured party wants to know the details of what happened. They want to know what the other man or woman looked like, where the two met, how the relationship grew, and what they did while they were

---

2   John S. Romanides, *The Ancestral Sin*, trans. George Gabriel (Ridgewood, NJ: Zephyr Publishing, 1998), p. 172.

3   Op. cit., p. 100.

together. The cheater never wants to talk about it. It's the same with confession. How many people love to rehearse all the ways they have cheated on their perfect relationship with God? And yet the cheater has to talk, has to relate the details the injured spouse wants to hear. It's the only way the air gets cleared.

So with you. What does the door of your church look like—the door you use when you go to church? Picture it in your mind. I never want you to walk through that door again without saying something to God about how you have cheated on Him since last time you were there. The door of your church, from now on, is the gateway of repentance for you. Only in this way will you understand why you're there in that building. In this way, church will begin to make sense to you.

And also schedule a time for confession with your priest or spiritual father.

The Atonement: It's a War

In the Scriptures, the struggle between God and the devil is sometimes described as a war—for instance, in the Book of Isaiah (14:12–15):

> How you are fallen from heaven,
> O Lucifer, son of the morning!
> How you are cut down to the ground,
> You who weakened the nations!
> For you have said in your heart:
> 'I will ascend into heaven,
> I will exalt my throne above the stars of God;
> I will also sit on the mount of the congregation
> On the farthest sides of the north;

I will ascend above the heights of the clouds,

I will be like the Most High.'

Yet you shall be brought down to Sheol,

To the lowest depths of the Pit."

And St. John says in his first epistle, "He who sins is of the devil, for the devil has sinned from the beginning. For this purpose the Son of God was manifested, that He might destroy the works of the devil" (1 John 3:8).

St. Paul tells us to dress every day as if we are in a war:

Therefore take up the whole armor of God, that you may be able to withstand in the evil day, and having done all, to stand. Stand therefore, having girded your waist with truth, having put on the breastplate of righteousness, and having shod your feet with the preparation of the gospel of peace; above all, taking the shield of faith with which you will be able to quench all the fiery darts of the wicked one. And take the helmet of salvation, and the sword of the Spirit, which is the word of God; praying always with all prayer and supplication in the Spirit, being watchful to this end with all perseverance and supplication for all the saints. (Eph. 6:13–20)

Picture yourself in a battle. You're creeping through a wooded area, looking for the enemy. Those with you are fighting on your side, on God's side. The unit moves slowly ahead, in a loose formation. Suddenly, one of the other soldiers loudly proclaims that he has decided to defect to the other side and starts shooting at you. You're wounded badly: "Demas has forsaken me, having loved this present world, and has departed for Thessalonica— Crescens for Galatia, Titus for Dalmatia. Only Luke is with me" (2 Tim. 4:10–11).

The enemy is easy to spot, when you can see him. But you don't see him often. The problem is that he persuades the soldiers in your unit to fire at each other. Sometimes they are sorry for what they've done, and sometimes they continue firing until they've killed people: "For false christs and false prophets will rise and show great signs and wonders to deceive, if possible, even the elect" (Matt. 24:24).

There are, thankfully, times when the opposite happens. Soldiers on the devil's side suddenly decide to transfer their allegiance, and they wreak havoc for the other army. Both sides have defectors, and both sides have become adept at welcoming back those who repent of their defection:

> And you *He made alive*, who were dead in trespasses and sins, in which you once walked according to the course of this world, according to the prince of the power of the air, the spirit who now works in the sons of disobedience, among whom also we all once conducted ourselves in the lusts of our flesh, fulfilling the desires of the flesh and of the mind, and were by nature children of wrath, just as the others. But God, who is rich in mercy, because of His great love with which He loved us, even when we were dead in trespasses, made us alive together with Christ. (Eph. 2:1–5)

But listen. I always want you to remember that you have a real advantage over those on the other side: *You know how the war is going to end.*

> And I saw the beast, the kings of the earth, and their armies, gathered together to make war against Him who sat on the horse and against His army. Then the beast was captured, and with him the false prophet who worked signs in his presence, by which he

deceived those who received the mark of the beast and those who worshiped his image. These two were cast alive into the lake of fire burning with brimstone. And the rest were killed with the sword which proceeded from the mouth of Him who sat on the horse. And all the birds were filled with their flesh. (Rev. 19:19–21)

That's pretty graphic, isn't it? "The birds were filled with their flesh." So with that in mind, ask yourself which side you want to be on. You switch sides continually, going from God's team to the devil's. We get tricked sometimes; we get wounded and the other side finds us first and takes care of us and sometimes we just think the devil's side looks like more fun. But eventually, what happens to everyone who takes that side? Bird food.

Remember this: One side wins and the other side loses. You might look around right now and ask yourself how it could possibly be true that God is going to win this war. Fr. John Romanides says it best: "For the present, many injustices and wrongs take place contrary to the will of God. God does not war against evil by force or by depriving creatures of freedom but by being long suffering through love and justice."[4] We have the promises of generations of God-lovers who have placed their faith in these promises. And we have the invitation to become a cosufferer with God as He is "long suffering through love and justice." At all times, the struggle between good and evil, between God and the devil, rages. The devil's army constantly attacks the children of God with the purpose of imposing his will on them.

In the same way you think of returning to the Father when you come into the church (as you walk in the door), I want you to imagine that when you leave the church through the same door, you go on patrol. Think Iraq or Afghanistan. You're going to put on your equipment, climb up on the

---

4   Romanides, op. cit., p. 75.

Humvee, and begin to drive the streets. You're totally focused on any indication that the enemy might be launching an attack. Sometimes it's a bullet, sometimes a roadside bomb. He has lots of tricks, but all of them result in the same thing: you get injured or die.

What is the equipment you carry?

- **The Scriptures:** "The sword of the Spirit . . . is the word of God" (Eph. 6:17).

- **Your prayer rope:** "Rejoice always, pray without ceasing, in everything give thanks; for this is the will of God in Christ Jesus for you" (1 Thess. 5:16–18).

- **Watchfulness:** "Be sober, be vigilant; because your adversary the devil walks about like a roaring lion, seeking whom he may devour" (1 Pet. 5:8).

The Devil

Have you noticed something about my two pictures of the atonement? The devil figures prominently in both of them. In fact, he figures more prominently in our lives than we care to admit. Why do we avoid admitting how much he influences us?

Unfortunately, much of what we think about the devil we get from popular culture. I don't want to talk about specific instances of the devil's appearance in pop culture—you know what they are. I only have to say this: When pop culture portrays the devil as a comic figure, it puts him on the same level as comic portrayals of other evil figures—Osama Bin Laden, Hitler, and the like. I have no problem with making Osama Bin Laden or Hitler look like fools, but I do have a problem with portraying the devil this way. When the devil is portrayed as comic, as a fool, or as a little guy standing on your shoulder opposite your guardian angel, he's really being portrayed as *manageable*.

Hitler, Muslim terrorists, and mass murderers cannot properly be portrayed as comic while they still wreak their destruction, but when they are ultimately overcome by good, they become ripe material for comic depictions. And why? It's because they have been revealed as manageable.

Is the devil manageable? Yes and no. I won't say he's unmanageable, but I will say that he's serious, and he has yet to be completely overwhelmed by good. As Christians we do not fear the devil, because we know that his power has already been broken. But we also realize that his craftiness has destroyed many people, families, churches, monasteries, communities, and even nations. That is not a comic figure. That is not someone you want to regard as manageable.

In addition to this, we don't want to admit to the place of the devil in our lives because it makes us sound like religious zealots, hillbilly preachers, or superstitious worrywarts. In an effort to avoid being associated with those kinds of groups, we avoid the Church's teaching concerning the devil.

We should not allow ourselves to be bullied into dropping important parts of our faith based on how we think others may view us. I recall one time when I was asked to preach at a church conference, and in my sermon, I said the name "Jesus" several times. Afterward, a man approached me and began mocking me—he said the name "Jesus" over and over in a kind of hillbilly accent. His priest told him later that his behavior was shameful, which it was. Can anyone claim to be a Christian who considers the name "Jesus" to be comical?

It's the same with the devil. If you think of the devil as comical, or manageable, then you're leaving yourself open to any attack he may launch. Imagine a war in which one side refuses to acknowledge the presence of the other side. What a slaughter that would be!

Remember how the devil played the role of agent in the fall of mankind in the third chapter of Genesis? Without his influence, mankind might have continued to live eternally in harmony with God—there is certainly nothing to indicate that either Adam or Eve was interested in disobeying God's one command before the devil suggested they do it.

> Now the serpent was more cunning than any beast of the field which the LORD God had made. And he said to the woman, "Has God indeed said, 'You shall not eat of every tree of the garden'?" And the woman said to the serpent, "We may eat the fruit of the trees of the garden; but of the fruit of the tree which *is* in the midst of the garden, God has said, 'You shall not eat it, nor shall you touch it, lest you die.'" Then the serpent said to the woman, "You will not surely die. For God knows that in the day you eat of it your eyes will be opened, and you will be like God, knowing good and evil." So when the woman saw that the tree was good for food, that it *was* pleasant to the eyes, and a tree desirable to make *one* wise, she took of its fruit and ate. She also gave to her husband with her, and he ate. (Gen. 3:1–6)

This event, which we know simply as the Fall, influenced all of human history. How? It touches our very lives by giving control of the world over to the devil. To quote Fr. Romanides: "As a result, this world which is in subjection to death and corruption cannot be considered natural, if by natural we mean the world as God intended it to be. In other words, the world is abnormal, but this is not because of its own nature but because a parasitic force exists in it at present."[5] We do not suffer the guilt of Adam's sin, but we suffer the consequences of the decision he made to hand the world over to the rule

---

5   Romanides, op. cit., p. 82.

of the devil. Everything you see around you at this moment is under his control, and by proclaiming yourself to belong to God's army you make yourself a counterinsurgent, a revolutionary, and a radical.

Just like our Lord. Jesus came into this world, to the camp of the evil one, and stole his most powerful weapons from him—suffering and death. Christ made those weapons His own: "For this purpose the Son of God was manifested, that He might destroy the works of the devil" (1 John 3:8). Our Lord walked into the enemy camp and swung their biggest cannons around so that they were pointing right at the devil. Brilliant!

God did not create death, nor was it His will that we should die: "For God did not make death / Neither does He have pleasure over the destruction of the living" (WSol. 1:13). "For God created man for immortality / And made him an image of His own eternity. / But death entered the world by the envy of the devil, / And those of his portion tempt it" (WSol. 2:23–24). As St. John Cassian says, "For the purpose of God whereby He made man not to perish but to live forever, stands immovable" (Conference 13, chapter 7).

This is God's will for you—that you would live forever. And love forever. It is the will of the devil that you would die, be separated from God, and never have even the tiniest experience of love. Can you see why I think it's important that we know why we're in church? When you understand the differences between good and evil, God and the devil, you run to church whenever you can. You return to the spouse who loves you. You rejoin the winning side, where you are loved, accepted, forgiven, and strengthened.

Think back to the young man I told you about at the beginning of this chapter—the high school dropout. He didn't understand the benefits of going to school, that's true. But hearing them, and even agreeing with them, did not make him want to go back. There had to be some other reason he had quit—something more than someone having said to him, "School is useless." I began to think he might have some learning disabilities that made regular classes difficult for him, and he had compensated by adopting a "who needs school anyway" attitude. But giving him information didn't get him back into school. We needed to go deeper and ask the question: What was getting through to him in his classes, and what was getting blocked by learning disabilities? That was the mystery we wanted to unlock.

It's exactly the same with us as we think about church. I hope this chapter has given you some necessary information about why people need the Church, but we haven't solved the problem yet. We need to drill down further into the question of "why go at all?" by thinking about our senses—what gets through, what gets blocked, and how distractions keep us from encountering God in the Church.

On a side note: We did indeed eventually persuade this young man to go back to high school, and he graduated. His life still had many significant challenges, but he had gained a high school diploma and a trade, and we showed him that anyone who puts his mind to something can accomplish great things. Isn't that true?

The Scriptures

I want you to notice something else about my explanation of the atonement: I rely heavily on the Scriptures. The word of God, as the Psalm tells us, is a light that guides us along the path of life (Ps. 119:105). You need that light. If you have the Scriptures as your constant companion, you can't go wrong— ask your priest for guidance in this.

In addition, as we address the problem of boredom by learning to control the mind, St. Isaac the Syrian tells us the Scriptures are one of the tools we cannot do without:

When a man's thoughts are totally immersed in the delight of pursuing the wisdom treasured in the words of Scripture by means of the faculty that extracts understanding from them, then he puts the world behind his back and forgets everything in it, and he blots out of his soul all memories that form images embodying the world. Often he does not even remember the employment of the habitual thoughts which visit human nature, and his soul remains in ecstasy by reason of those new encounters that arise from the sea of the Scripture's mysteries.[6]

---

6   *The Ascetical Homilies of St. Isaac the Syrian* (Boston: Holy Transfiguration Monastery, 2011), pp. 115–116.

Chapter Three

The Divine Liturgy

I HAVE SPOKEN WITH PEOPLE who think there is an easy solution to the problem that church is sometimes boring. They say we should simply do what other churches do: Make the service shorter. Have a drama or some dancers. Make the music more exciting. Tell more jokes.

I don't know what to say to this, especially when an Orthodox person is making the suggestion. I feel like we've almost lost that person. His concept of what it means to worship God has deteriorated to such a degree that we cannot speak the same spiritual language anymore. Is it really possible to take the atmosphere of a comedy club or a stadium concert into the church and expect that our worship of God will not change? *Change* really isn't a strong enough word here. Can we imagine our worship of God would not be destroyed? Look back at history and see examples of how the changing of *one word* in the creed or in the translation of Scripture has opened giant rifts between ancient churches. One word! One thought! One nuance of theology! The tiniest division in one century becomes an insurmountable rupture in the next.

Those who want to make church "more exciting" have lost the perspective of history. If church attendance is dropping off, they reason, then a few modifications will bring the crowds in and we'll be back on track. No! They need to ask themselves: What will the Church need to do twenty years from now to entertain people enough to get them to come? What will the Church have to do one hundred years from now, or three hundred? If you want the Church to become a media corporation in order to boost attendance, what is the long-term significance of that decision?

And yes, I've had people say to me that Christ will come back before the Church is destroyed by its addiction to entertainment. I can't disagree with this argument, because our Lord could come back at any time. But I can say, Are we really going to jeopardize the future of the Church by presuming upon the Second Coming of Christ? Have not people throughout history done this, to their own shame and to the harm of future generations?

Not you. You understand that the Church must remain. Times of persecution will come to this land eventually, and when they do, Christians will need a serious Church that is able to provide a refuge for us. We have to have a place where we can worship God in the beauty of holiness, not in compromise and foolishness.

So what does this mean for you? It means that the Church is not going to change, but you can. If you find yourself occasionally bored in the Divine Liturgy, you're going to find some way of addressing that head on. You know you're bored when nothing important seems to be happening and everybody's just waiting for the next part of the service. Everyone wants to "get on with it," mostly so they can go home. But we can't just get on with it, because that's not what the service books say, or the Typicon (a guidebook that tells the priest and chanter/choir how the service should go), or the bishop.

Boredom starts with the senses. It's an emotion, but it starts in your senses. You're standing in church—the chanter/choir is singing, or the priest is preaching—and you begin to think it's dragging a little, so your senses tell your mind to go someplace interesting. Your mind takes off like a mouse released from its cage. Once it does that, it never comes back, and you spend the rest of the service bored. Except, let's say, when an altar server drops a candle or a kid whacks his head against a pew and starts screaming—or something else happens to distract you that really has nothing to do with worshiping God.

Remember where this process started? The senses. Let's think about that for a moment. Since the time of Descartes, the French philosopher who is the father of all modern philosophy and science, we have been encouraged to look to our senses to tell us what is true or not. This revolution resulted in many important advances for mankind because it ushered in the age of scientific method. But it also poisoned the faith of those who began to rely on their senses as the final authority in spiritual matters. Some said to themselves, *I have never seen a man rise from the dead after three days, so Christ did not rise from the dead.* Or, *I don't understand how God can be Three in One and One in Three, so it must be a fallacy.* Or, *Virgins can't give birth, so Mary was not a virgin when she gave birth to Christ.*

These are examples of how people are led astray by their senses. Or, more accurately, how people are led astray by applying the scientific method to spiritual things. Do you really want to say that your senses provide you with perfect information, information you will trust even with your eternal soul? There are two reasons this is a really bad idea.

The first reason is pointed out in Scripture. When St. Paul was describing the power of the gospel to the Corinthian church, he told them that, no matter who they were, the mercies of God were too great for them to comprehend: "For Jews request a sign, and Greeks seek after wisdom; but we preach Christ crucified, to the Jews a stumbling block and to the Greeks foolishness, but to those who are called, both Jews and Greeks, Christ the power of God and the wisdom of God" (1 Cor. 1:22–24). See what he's saying? Jewish theology emphasized historical events and people, but the incarnate God coming to this world to suffer and die was too radical an event for them to understand. The Greeks were interested in philosophy, but what philosophy would talk about the Crucifixion as the supreme expression of the wisdom of God? It makes no sense.

And yet that's what God did. We hadn't even asked for forgiveness, but He made it available to us. We didn't seek Him, but He sought us. By sinning, we gave ourselves over to death, but He took death and made it a gateway to His eternal Kingdom. How can you explain something like that philosophically? If you rely on your senses, on the rules of human logic, it's impossible. The words *wisdom of God* say it all. God has a wisdom we do not have.

Do you think, then, that when you stand in the worship of the Most High God, celebrating His forbearance and love, you should rely on your senses to tell you whether it's *interesting* or not? Even in the times when the Scriptures were being written, St. Paul knew there would be people for whom the gospel made no sense at all. God loves me the way I am? God forgives me, and all I have to do is ask? It didn't seem possible. St. Paul needed to remind people constantly that this is exactly what Jesus Christ did for us.

We cannot say we believe *because* of our feelings, but more often than not we believe *in spite* of them:

The beginning of a man's true life is the fear of God. But the fear of God will not be persuaded to dwell in a soul together with distraction over outward things. For by serving the senses, the heart is scattered, driven away from delight in God; for our inward thoughts, it is said, are bound by their perception to the sensory organs that serve them.[7]

But there's more. Our senses are not the only enemy we have. In the same way that our senses are not a good indication of what is truthful, our reason tends to lead us astray as well. Let's explore this by taking a brief look at some brilliant teachers in the history of the Church: Origin, Arius, and Nestorius—our most famous heretics.

Origen lived in the second and third century. He was the first Christian to write extensively about theology and Scripture, and he was the leader of a large school of Christianity in Alexandria (and elsewhere when Alexandria became inhospitable to him). I'm not going to go into the life or theology of Origen; you can research that yourself if you want to. But I'll say this: Origen asked himself questions that fueled his theological thought, such as: What was the cosmos like before mankind was created? What will happen at the very end of time? How was Christ the Son the agent of Creation, and what does this tell us about His relation to God the Father? And so on.

Some three hundred years after Origen died, people who were devotees of his writings started to proclaim heresies that were condemned by an ecumenical council. Origen was condemned right along with them (when you're dead it's difficult to explain, defend, or change your teaching). With the pages and pages of commentary and speculation he produced, it's understandable that some of it would be a little shaky. A little questionable. A little *too* speculative.

How does that relate to us and to our feeling that church is occasionally boring? The battle not only takes place in the senses; it also takes place in the

---

7   St. Isaac the Syrian, *op cit.*, pp. 114–115.

mind. When you stand in church and your mind starts wandering around, you're going to get into trouble. Even when it wanders in seemingly "religious" directions but is no longer focused on God Himself, you're navigating dangerous and deadly waters.

Arius is a great example of this. Ordained later in life, he was a devoted opponent of the prevailing heresies of the day. And yet he asked himself a question that got him into trouble: How can Christ be co-eternal with God the Father? Co-eternal seems so undefined and mysterious. Arius didn't think it should be that way. He wanted a Christian theology that was clean, defined, and enlightened. He began to teach the heresy that Christ the Son, the Second Person of the Trinity, was created by God. He denied the co-eternity of Christ.

Arius got the chance Origen never got—he was condemned as a heretic during his lifetime and was given the opportunity to repent. Did he repent? Probably not, although we'll never know, because he died while he was on the way to (supposedly) make a public proclamation of repentance. (He died in a particularly gruesome manner similar to several notable enemies of God, which is one reason the sincerity of his repentance is doubtful.)

See where I'm going with this? Both of these men were intelligent and were part of the Church. Both of them wanted to know and serve God. But both of them went astray by telling themselves they could wrap their minds around God.

Now, don't think I'm saying that all intelligent people become heretics or that writing theology automatically leads to heresy. No. I'm making a point about you and me, when we stand in church and sometimes say to ourselves, "This is boring." Is it heretical to say such a thing? No, but it's reasonable. Yes, I said "reasonable." There is no other word that so accurately describes the heretics of the Church. They embraced intellectual dissatisfaction. They wanted to invent something new. They wanted to solve problems that did not exist. They wanted to wrap their minds around God.

One writer said this about another of the early heretics, Nestorius: "the unfortunate Nestorius, whose chief error, in retrospect, appears to have been pedantic exactitude."[8] That tells me Nestorius said to himself, "I'm not going to take things the way they've been given to me. I want to think more, and discover more, and then force other people to believe what I've thought and what I've discovered."

Not good. Everyone who writes anything in the Church, or who preaches a sermon, or who even makes his opinion known to a friend at coffee hour, must take great care to fit snugly into the traditions the Church has given us. If you want to map new territory, you should understand that (1) someone has already done it, and (2) it's heresy.

Here's how I like to look at it. I have a guy who fixes my cars. I've been going to him for years. I trust him. I've gone to other guys, and I've either paid too much or discovered that, after they "fixed" my car, it was not fixed at all. My guy does not do that. He charges me a fair price, and he's a mechanical genius. When I drive away from his shop, I know that I don't need to worry at all about the thing he's fixed. It's fixed.

All of us need someone we can trust when it comes to our cars. Or health, or taxes, or teeth, or child care, or whatever. There are parts of your life you cannot handle yourself, and you need to hand over control to someone else. Of course, if you want to fill your own cavities, go ahead. Have fun!

It's the same with your spiritual life. When you walk into church, when you begin to hear the music and words of the Divine Liturgy, you are really handing over control of your soul to—whom? In whom exactly are you putting your trust? I'll tell you: You're handing the care of your soul over to

8   Harold Brown, OJ, *Heresies* (Peabody, MA: Hendrickson Publishers, 1998), p. 174.

our Lord Jesus Christ, the apostles, the saints, the bishops, the martyrs, the priests. To all the saints who have lived before you, who have stood in church in exactly the same way you're standing in church, and have experienced the salvation and renewal of their souls. To the martyrs who have died to make sure you have the Church as a spiritual home.

We need someone we can trust. We can't trust our senses, and we can't trust our minds. But we can trust the vehicle by which thousands, millions, of people have worshiped and communicated with God—the Divine Liturgy of the Great Church.

Doesn't this sound wonderful? As we stand in church, we can almost see (without putting absolute trust in our senses) the glories of the worship of God. And when He reaches into our hearts in the Holy Eucharist, we understand His love for us.

But there are also times when all this dissolves, and we look around and see empty seats, people not paying attention, kids screaming to get out of the church. Frankly, it's sometimes difficult to see how, by way of the Divine Liturgy on earth, we participate in the eternal Liturgy in the heavenly Kingdom. The earthly part sometimes seems to overwhelm the heavenly part.

Is there something we're not seeing here?

Chapter Four

What You See Is Not What You Get

WHEN I WAS IN HIGH SCHOOL, I got invited to a cast party after a show I was in. I agreed to go.

As soon as I walked in the door, it was immediately clear to me that somewhere another cast party was going on. The scene before me had the feeling of a children's birthday party—a *poorly attended* children's birthday party. A few kids were sitting in the living room while the host's mom served drinks—you could choose punch or soda. Broadway music was playing on a radio in the dining room, which was filled with cupcakes and bowls of potato chips. I was not really close friends with any of the kids who were there; in fact, it seemed like none of them were close friends with anyone, because they were all sitting there in complete silence.

I had stumbled into an *out*cast party. I had gone because it was being held at the home of a friend of mine. She was intent on having the cast party at her house, but "no one" went because they knew it would be—like it was. I stayed because I felt sorry for her. I sat there dreaming of running out of the house, jumping into a car, and driving to where the good party was happening.

Have you ever walked into church and noticed all the ways the people there do not measure up to your standards? Your mind says to you, *Hey! Don't you wonder where all the fun people are? They're not here, that's for sure!*

Maybe you notice how the choir, the icons, or the priest do not quite meet your expectations? *Wow, the choir sounds terrible, but it's okay, it will be over soon enough.* Or perhaps you compare the gathering of the faithful in church to other gatherings—sports, entertainment, business—and determine that church really doesn't have the pizzazz these other things have. *Lots of churches are closing their doors—perhaps this one is on its last legs too.*

We all tend to judge based on appearances. We see the bad in things unless we expect something different. And we want to be where quality is. Some chase after the crowds, and some avoid the crowds—that's not what I'm talking about. I mean that each of us, flashy or quiet, wants to feel good about ourselves and the group we identify with.

I always found that when people made fun of religion or mocked me because of my faith, I didn't really care. Anyone who does that is worth my time only in that I feel sorry for them. But it really hurt when people who were a part of the Church lacked enthusiasm, when people who were part of my group just didn't seem to have the commitment I had. These were people who believed in what the Church taught; they just didn't think it was a big deal. They didn't care. On the occasions I would see this kind of person in church, it made the place seem tired, old, dowdy, and empty—like there was another party happening somewhere else, and I wished I was there.

There are reasons this may happen in your church that are outside your control. You can't make the priest speak clearly; you can't teach the choir to sing (or if you can, you'd better volunteer your services as voice coach); you can't tell the old lady next to you that just because her perfume was on sale this week, she didn't need to bathe in it. Or what about your friends who are simply not there, who have no concern for their spiritual lives? What can you do? Nothing, really.

But there is something that's not outside your control, and that's your

mind. Let's look at a story from Scripture to see the different directions people's minds wander when they're standing in the same place. It's from Luke
18:10–14:

> Two men went up to the temple to pray, one a Pharisee and the
> other a tax collector. The Pharisee stood and prayed thus with him-
> self, "God, I thank You that I am not like other men—extortioners,
> unjust, adulterers, or even as this tax collector. I fast twice a week;
> I give tithes of all that I possess." And the tax collector, standing
> afar off, would not so much as raise *his* eyes to heaven, but beat
> his breast, saying, "God, be merciful to me a sinner!" I tell you,
> this man went down to his house justified *rather* than the other; for
> everyone who exalts himself will be humbled, and he who humbles
> himself will be exalted.

This passage primarily addresses the subject of repentance, but it also
has something to say about where you put your mind, and your eyes, while
you're in church.

The Pharisee's mind was on himself. His goal in coming to worship God
was to feel good about himself. I can't tell you how many times people have
said this to me—and I mean good people speaking genuinely about what
brings them to church. I suppose they say, "I go to church because it makes
me feel good," because they think it makes me happy to hear that. "You're
doing a great job, Father! I feel good when I go to church!" Let me ask you:
In the parable of the Pharisee and the tax collector, who felt good and who
did not? If you want an example of someone from Scripture who attends the
worship of God in order to feel good, it's definitely the Pharisee in Luke 18.
He is our model for going to church in order to feel good. And what a terrible model he is!

But that wasn't the only problem the Pharisee had. His eyes also conspired against him to destroy his soul, just as much as his mind—or his feelings—did. As he stood in the worship of the Most High God, his eyes wandered around, judging the people he saw. Looking at them, assessing them. Comparing himself to them. He liked to do this because when he put himself up against the other people, he felt like the top dog. And why not? He was proud of himself—why wouldn't God be proud of him?

Do you spend your time in church looking around at the other people in order to compare yourself to them? This, brothers and sisters, is a bad idea. Your only companion from Scripture is the Pharisee, and by extension, the devil—and both of them hate you.

Let's look at the tax collector. He had only one thing to say when he came to worship God: "God, be merciful to me, a sinner!" As this man considered God and prayed to God, he encountered God. The Pharisee did not; in fact, I think that's why the text says he "prayed thus with himself." The Pharisee prayed to a god he had created in his own image. The tax collector, on the other hand, could sense in his soul that God's exceeding goodness stood in direct contrast to his sin. Therefore, wanting to commune in some meaningful way with God, he cried out for forgiveness.

Where were his eyes? "And the tax collector, standing afar off, would not so much as raise his eyes to heaven." There is a good reason our Lord and St. Luke include this sentence in this story. It's important for you to know where the tax collector kept his eyes—on himself. He would not judge anyone. He would not compare himself to anyone. In fact, he did not even see anyone else besides himself and God. He knew that, in order to guard his mind, he needed first to guard his eyes. The sentence says he "would" not raise his eyes. If I say, "This man *didn't* raise his eyes," I'm making a statement of fact. But if I say, "He *wouldn't* raise his eyes," I imply something more: an amount of willpower, a decision, even stubbornness. The tax collector was stubborn: he would not follow the promptings of his mind, his curiosity, or the voice of the devil telling him to lighten up and enjoy the service.

Try keeping your eyes away from judging other people the next time you're in church. It's very difficult. Judging the people around you is the thing that, unless you think about it constantly, your eyes do naturally when left to themselves.

Look at how the story ends. The Pharisee goes to his home humbled, and the tax collector exalted. These words, *exalted* and *humbled*, refer to the reward these men have received for attending the worship of God. The Pharisee walks away humbled: sad, depressed, head hung low, condemned, dragging himself along the ground (perhaps "dragging" is an exaggeration, but you know what I mean). The tax collector walks away in exactly the way I want *you* to walk away from church the next time you're there: lifted up, joyous, redeemed, justified, floating a few inches above the ground (well, figuratively). When your time in church is spent in repentance and communion with God, your heart will be overflowing with joy when you walk out.

This is why I say, "What you see is *not* what you get." When you look around during the Divine Liturgy, you will be able to find a thousand ways in which it does not look like God is present there at all. It does not look like a participation in the heavenly Divine Liturgy served at the throne of God and attended by the angels. It may not even look spiritual. But it is. That's the promise the Church makes to you, I make to you, God makes to you. The Divine Liturgy has a power and glory your eyes may not see. Angels are there, and you do not see them. Christ is present, and you don't see Him either.

Another great passage speaks to the issue of what we see with our eyes. It's from John 1:47–51:

Jesus saw Nathanael coming toward Him, and said of him, "Behold, an Israelite indeed, in whom is no deceit!" Nathanael said to Him, "How do You know me?" Jesus answered and said to him, "Before Philip called you, when you were under the fig tree, I saw you." Nathanael answered and said to Him, "Rabbi, You are the Son of God! You are the King of Israel!" Jesus answered and said to him, "Because I said to you, 'I saw you under the fig tree,' do you believe? You will see greater things than these." And He said to him, "Most assuredly, I say to you, hereafter you shall see heaven open, and the angels of God ascending and descending upon the Son of Man."

At first reading, this passage makes Nathaniel seem a little simple-minded. Did he really come to believe in Jesus because Jesus saw him sitting under a fig tree? No. This is not what happened. Rather, we see here that Nathaniel's tendency, like that of many people, was to judge others quickly. Remember that just a few verses before, when Philip told Nathaniel about Jesus, he mentioned Jesus was from Nazareth. Nathanael asked him, "Can anything good come out of Nazareth?" (1:46). Do you see what he was doing? He judged Jesus without meeting him at all. He judged him based only on where He was from.

But something changed when he actually met our Lord. As soon as Nathaniel spoke to Jesus, he judged Jesus very differently. In fact, he may have been like a number of people in St. John's Gospel who, upon meeting Jesus, instantly knew He was God Incarnate. But that's not the (only) point. The point is that Nathaniel's eyes had not been opened to all that Jesus would show him: the miracles, the teachings, the Crucifixion, and ultimately, the Resurrection. Jesus told him he would, if he remained as a disciple, see these "greater things." All he had seen to that point was Jesus, the man, standing there before him, and for whatever reason, he made a snap judgment and called Jesus the King of Israel.

Nathaniel was like a large percentage of people in church today. Many have taken the quick look, made a snap judgment, and decided that Jesus is their Savior. But that's not what our Lord wants. Not at all. He wants you and me to "see heaven open, and the angels of God ascending and descending upon the Son of Man" (1:51). He knows the snap judgment is just as likely to go against the Church as it is to go in favor of the Church. If you've built your membership in the Church on a "Nathaniel" basis, a faith that is not well thought-out, then you're rather likely to leave if something better comes along.

On the other hand, if you can see with the eyes of your heart those things that our Lord promised Nathaniel, then your commitment to God will be solid and true, and your spirit strong.

How does this work, practically speaking? To answer this, we're going to look at the word *hope* as it's defined by Scripture. Let's look at Romans 5:3–5: "And not only *that*, but we also glory in tribulations, knowing that tribulation produces perseverance; and perseverance, character; and character, hope. Now hope does not disappoint, because the love of God has been poured out in our hearts by the Holy Spirit who was given to us." What does St. Paul want us to have hope about? Our salvation. The future. Hope is always about the future. You don't hope for something if you already have it; you hope for something you haven't gotten yet (Rom. 8:24–25).

St. Paul reminds the Romans (and us) that the things they see and experience in this world are transitory: "For I consider that the sufferings of this present time are not worthy *to be compared* with the glory which shall be revealed in us" (8:18). In other words, he reminds them that, when they look around and it appears that God is not present—it appears that there is no salvation—they must lean on the promises of God.

Then St. Paul takes it a step further. We are not the only ones who are eagerly hoping in the promises of God—all of creation is: "For the earnest expectation of the creation eagerly waits for the revealing of the sons of God" (8:19). All creation waits for the same things we do—salvation and the restoration of all things.

The reason the creation dares to hope for restoration is the Incarnation of God. God came to us in a divine Body, and because the body was God's, it was just as divine as He was and is. Jesus was not divine only in some areas but not in others—it's a kind of heresy to say that. Not only was His soul divine, but His body was divine as well. His feet and hands and blood and fingernails—all divine.

The fact that God came to this world in a human body gave hope to all of creation. Until that point, creation was imprisoned by the sin of Adam. He got the earth as a gift from God and promptly handed it over to the devil. But when Christ came, He brought the creation back into the possession of God. He stole the earth back from the devil and restored it to its former glory. Look outside at a tree. Was that tree (not that particular one; I mean trees in general) different before Christ came than after? Absolutely! Before Christ came, that tree belonged to the devil; at the Resurrection of Christ it became God's. So yes, it was very different.

But also—no, it really wasn't different. Same bark, same roots, same leaves. Did all the trees suddenly *look* different after the Resurrection? Not at all. The difference is that now, since the Incarnation of Christ, the creation has hope. We can't see that. But we can trust God and His word. He made creation: "By faith we understand that the worlds were framed by the word of God, so that the things which are seen were not made of things which are visible" (Heb. 11:3). I like the poetry of those words, but I'm tempted to paraphrase them: "The things you see were not created by things you can see." And in addition, they've been redeemed, but you can't see that either. Their redemption is not yet complete.

Think of it this way. At the Resurrection, our Lord pushed the devil off a cliff. He hasn't hit the stones at the bottom yet, but he will. That's a picture of hope. Your hope, not the devil's. He doesn't have any hope. He's going to hit the stones; it's a sure thing, but it hasn't happened just yet.

Now, back to the Divine Liturgy. A kid bonked his head against a pew and is screaming, and the mom won't take him out of the church. Until that point, you were starting to enjoy the Liturgy, to pray, to feel good about being in church. But not anymore. Now no one can hear anything, and the noise is throwing the choir off pitch enough that you're almost glad you can't hear them. What happened? Were the angels there in the church at the beginning, and then did they fly off to another church when the distractions began? How outrageous. The angels are still there. Do they leave when the Liturgy goes on too long or when the sermon has a multitude of words but no point? Preposterous.

Here's why you should go to church: because you get way more than you bargained for. The Church is the point in the universe where God is most present, and let me give you this advice: I think you'd be the most happy you'll ever be when you're consistently in that place. What you see is not what you get—you get way more than you can see. Look around at the icons, and embrace that hope that tells you those saints are with you right at that moment, and praying for you.

One time I had the experience of carrying a myrrh-gushing icon in a procession. It had not gushed myrrh for some time before the service that day. As I was carrying it with another priest, the icon started gushing myrrh. I remember looking down at my hand, because I could feel that it had become wet. I wondered how it got wet—I'm being honest with you now; I didn't even think about the possibility that it was the icon. My hand felt oily, and when I held it up to my face to look closer it had an overwhelming smell of beauty. Holiness. Only then did I notice that the icon was streaming myrrh.

We had processed around the outside of the church and had stopped to do a prayer right on the sidewalk in the front. As the priest was praying, I looked across the street, and—again, I'm being honest with you— the thought popped into my head, *Why doesn't the stop sign over there ever gush myrrh? Or the cars going by?* In other words, it had struck me that I was holding in my hand a gateway to the eternal, to the holy. We had been given a unique privilege of actually seeing (and smelling) the glory of God. And where did that happen? In a mall, in an office, on the street outside a hair salon? Of course not! It happened in the church. The church is the place of miracles. All the miracles that occur outside the church originate in the church, because the church is the house of the originator of miracles.

Remember the outcast party from the beginning of the chapter? I have to tell you, as sad as it was at the beginning, that's how much fun it was by the end. It took a little while for everybody to get warmed up, but they did eventually, and it was a great party. I was correct that there was another party, and that other one apparently got a little out of hand. At some point the police were called, and a number of the kids who had gone to that party ran away and came to our party. Some of the kids who *didn't* leave had drugs on them when the police showed up. What a mess! In the following days and weeks, as we found out how much trouble these kids were in (this was the seventies, remember), over and over again I thanked God that I had stayed at the outcast party.

Look around you while you're in church, not to judge those who are also there, but to help your mind understand that the church is a holy place. Your mind might occasionally whine like an annoying child that it wants to go to a different party. Tell it to be quiet. Look around you. You are exactly where you are supposed to be.

he Flesh of God

I WANT TO TELL YOU A STORY about a time when nearly all of Jesus' disciples left Him. I'm not talking about the trial and Crucifixion. I'm talking about another time.

Our Lord had a large number of people following Him, and they all believed in Him. They wanted to be His disciples. He began to teach them one day, and—unbelievably—almost all of them were so *disgusted* by what He said, they decided they didn't want to follow Him after all. So many people left Him that day that our Lord turned to the Twelve, the inner circle of His disciples, and asked them if they wanted to leave Him too. They said no.

What could Jesus possibly have said that would make almost all His disciples leave Him? Let's go through the story bit by bit (John 6:30–71).

> Therefore they said to Him, "What sign will You perform then, that
> we may see it and believe You? What work will You do? Our fathers
> ate the manna in the desert; as it is written, '*He gave them bread from
> heaven to eat*.'" Then Jesus said to them, "Most assuredly, I say to
> you, Moses did not give you the bread from heaven, but My Father

gives you the true bread from heaven. For the bread of God is He who comes down from heaven and gives life to the world." Then they said to Him, "Lord, give us this bread always." (vv. 30–34)

This passage starts out with people following Jesus—almost stalking Him—because of the miracle of the loaves and the fishes in John 6:1–14 (the beginning of the same chapter). What did this miracle mean to them? I tell you what it *should* have meant to them: it should have meant that our Lord could create something out of nothing. The bread did not exist, but He created it. It was real. It filled the stomachs of the people who ate it. And the miracle should have pointed them to a greater truth—that is, the continuing presence of Christ's Body and Blood in the Eucharist. But no. The message they took from this miracle was: If you follow Jesus, you get free food.

They wanted free food. They wanted to find Him and stick with Him like glue, because they would not have to work any longer. Notice at the beginning of the quotation above they wanted Jesus to do another miracle—and guess what? They had a suggestion about the miracle He might choose. "Our fathers ate the manna in the desert; as it is written, 'He gave them bread from heaven to eat.'" They wanted to offer a good theological argument for Jesus giving them more free food. After all, God did it in the desert, right? And not just once. You can almost hear them say, "That was great that you did the miracle with the bread, Jesus. But we're hungry again. If you really want to be the Son of God, you'll do that miracle every day. If you do, we'll make you our king!"

Our Lord agreed with them. Certainly, He told them, they would have access to the Bread that comes from heaven every day of their lives (vv. 32–33). Notice their response. They were happy. Perhaps a couple of them had brought baskets to take some loaves back to their family: "Jesus? Could

I take a couple loaves back to my mother? She didn't come today because her sciatica is acting up." They thought He had agreed to a repeat performance.

Our Lord offered a clarification: "And Jesus said to them, 'I am the bread of life. He who comes to Me shall never hunger, and he who believes in Me shall never thirst'" (v. 35). I can almost imagine our Lord touched His chest with His index finger while saying these words. "Do you want the Bread of Life? It's Me. I Myself am the Bread of Life."

With these words, the people started to get angry. They started to think that Jesus was stonewalling them—that is, He might have been delaying the miracle because He really couldn't do it. "The Jews then complained about Him, because He said, 'I am the bread which came down from heaven.' And they said, 'Is not this Jesus, the son of Joseph, whose father and mother we know? How is it then that He says, "I have come down from heaven"?'" (vv. 41–42). At this point in the story, the crowd was beginning to understand Christ's words. They were beginning to realize He might not give them free food as He had done the day before.

This was part of our Lord's response: "Most assuredly, I say to you, he who believes in Me has everlasting life. I am the bread of life. Your fathers ate the manna in the wilderness, and are dead. This is the bread which comes down from heaven, that one may eat of it and not die. I am the living bread which came down from heaven. If anyone eats of this bread, he will live forever; and the bread that I shall give is My flesh, which I shall give for the life of the world" (vv. 47–51). I want you to imagine that our Lord points to Himself as He says these words, even perhaps that He pinches a little bit of the skin on the back of His hand as He says, "this bread."

Now, let's pause for a moment and consider what our Lord was saying to the people who were listening that day, and to us. He says that His actual body is literally the Bread that was sent from heaven. Not a symbol. Not a metaphor. Nothing like that. That's why I want you to picture Him pointing to Himself, or pinching a little bit of His skin between His fingers. His words are literal.

How do I know that? I know it because of the response of the people listening to Him. These were people who wanted to believe in Him. They were listening to His words and paying attention. If they had responded to our Lord as if His words were metaphorical, I would agree with those who say He was speaking metaphorically. But they didn't: "The Jews therefore quarreled among themselves, saying, 'How can this Man give us *His* flesh to eat?'" (v. 52). And later: "Therefore many of His disciples, when they heard *this*, said, 'This is a hard saying; who can understand it?'" (v. 60).

This is a hard saying. We have a great blessing in that we are able to partake of the Body and Blood of Christ on a regular basis. Sometimes we see a Divine Liturgy that doesn't really seem to express the glory of the event that is taking place. But listen. The disciples were shocked precisely because our Lord said so clearly that His flesh would become their food: "For My flesh is food indeed, and My blood is drink indeed" (v. 55).

Our Lord started teaching this central truth of our faith to those who had followed Him, those who wanted to see a repeat of the free-food miracle. But He continued to teach His disciples when the crowd had gone away, and even His disciples found the teaching repulsive: "From that *time* many of His disciples went back and walked with Him no more" (v. 66). This was a different group from the crowd in the beginning of the passage. These were not people who followed Christ only for food, or for the promise of food. These were part of the group of followers whom St. John identified as "disciples." They had decided to follow Jesus, but when He started to teach them about the Eucharist, they left Him.

Only the Twelve remained with Him: "Then Jesus said to the twelve,

'Do you also want to go away?' But Simon Peter answered Him, 'Lord, to whom shall we go? You have the words of eternal life. Also we have come to believe and know that You are the Christ, the Son of the living God'" (vv. 67–69). This must have been a very difficult time. Up until that day, Jesus' popularity had soared, and crowds followed Him everywhere He went. But then He said a few words and nearly everyone left Him.

How about you? Do you believe our Lord spoke the truth when He said these words? He tells us that in the Eucharist we actually eat His Body and drink His Blood. The Body and Blood of God. Do you think it's a mostly symbolic ceremony? Ask yourself: Did the people in John 6 think Jesus was speaking symbolically? Not a chance—that's why they left Him. In their thinking, He was describing cannibalism. Would they have stopped following someone they believed in if He had told them to perform a ritual in which they symbolically ate the body and drank the blood of God? And in addition to that, don't you think our Lord would have stopped them as they walked away from Him? Wouldn't He have loved them enough to clarify His words, to explain to them that He was speaking symbolically so they would return and enjoy salvation? Certainly He would have, if His words were indeed symbolic. But they weren't.

This is why I think it's such a big deal to go to church. Listen to this: "Then Jesus said to them, 'Most assuredly, I say to you, unless you eat the flesh of the Son of Man and drink His blood, you have no life in you'" (v. 53). That's very serious to my way of thinking. We are not able on this side of heaven to understand why we must partake of the Eucharist in order to have a spiritual life, but I can tell you one thing: that's what our Lord said, and I, for one, am putting my trust in His words.

So when I say that even if church is sometimes boring, it's worth the effort to change our hearts so that we benefit from being there, I'm saying it because there is a treasure of infinite value in the Church, something which saves your soul and which you can get nowhere else on earth.

Again I say to you: Don't you think it's worth the effort? Since it's worth the effort to be in church in the first place, let's begin to look straight at the problem of boredom in order to overcome it. Our first question will be: What is it that makes us bored in church?

Part II

But What If I'm Bored in Church?

Chapter Six

Six Reasons
You May Find Church Boring

1. It's Not Good Entertainment

A passage from the book *St. Innocent, Apostle to America* tells us about people seeing a Divine Liturgy for the first time:

> The first real breakthrough towards converting these people came only in 1837, when Fr. John visited Fort Dionysius east of Sitka on the American coast. There, outside the compound walls, in a latticed enclosure he celebrated Divine Liturgy for the first time. He informed the local Tlingits of the service well in advance, and some 1500 of them assembled for the occasion. The respect and decorum with which they watched this new and incomprehensible spectacle amazed Fr. John and earned them his respect. He recalls: ". . . not only the adults, but even the children made no noise whatsoever, nor did they do anything unseemly during the service, which lasted more than an hour."[9]

9   Paul D. Garrett, *St. Innocent, Apostle to America* (Crestwood, NY: St. Vladimir's Seminary Press, 1979), pp. 109–110.

A couple of things amaze me about this passage. First, St. Innocent (Fr. John was his name when he was a priest; he took the name Innocent when he became a bishop) used the Divine Liturgy as his way of evangelizing the native people. No explanation, no videos, no handouts, no nothing. He just invited a large group of people to the celebration of the Divine Liturgy and let the Liturgy speak for itself. And guess what? Many of the people who were there that day became Christians.

The next time you're in church, imagine you're there for the first time. Imagine you've never seen a Liturgy before. What about the Divine Liturgy would make you say, "This is definitely the faith I want for myself and my family"? That's what happened that day in Alaska, when the future Saint Innocent celebrated the Liturgy east of Sitka.

The other thing that catches my eye in this passage is the author's use of the words "incomprehensible spectacle." That's quite a description! Sounds like my golf game—but we won't get into that. I think it's a great description of the Liturgy in the book. The indigenous people who were present that day could not understand the words of the Liturgy, so it *was* incomprehensible. And yet their hearts told them the truth was being proclaimed. This raises a question we will examine later: Do you really have to understand everything in the Liturgy in order to know that it proclaims the truth?

And it was a spectacle as well. A spectacle is something that captures people's attention. Now, I am really against anyone viewing the Divine Liturgy as entertainment. And yet I also work very hard to make sure the celebration of the Liturgy in my parish is beautiful, organized, and memorable. Can I add the word *entertaining*? Only for those who don't yet understand it.

If someone walks into the church for the first time and we're celebrating the Divine Liturgy, that person naturally focuses on the externals of what he sees and hears. He sees the icons, hears the music and the words, smells the incense. But I fully expect that, when that same person attends the Liturgy again and again, he will begin to explore the deeper meanings of Christian worship and come closer to understanding the Liturgy as a bridge between himself and God—and not as entertainment.

Guess what? The Divine Liturgy is not a form of entertainment. If you view it that way, even by mistake (or because you've never analyzed your attitude toward the Liturgy), you're going to miss the eternal benefits the Liturgy offers. In addition, you're probably not going to enjoy being in church. If the Church celebrates the Liturgy in order to be entertaining, it's not working. There are better ways—everywhere in our society, even on the tiny screens of cell phones—to be entertained.

I want you to learn to regard the Divine Liturgy in an entirely different way.

2. What Language Is That, Anyway?

A long time ago, I received an invitation to go to a church on its feast day, which fell on a Saturday. The priest told me, "There will be more people than on Pascha!"

"Okay," I said, "I'll come."

When I arrived at the church, he handed me a copy of the book he used for the Divine Liturgy. It was in a language I didn't speak, understand, or read. I informed him of this fact, and he looked at me as if I had just told him I wanted to celebrate the Liturgy with a parrot on my shoulder. I told him I would be able to use my own Liturgy book without any trouble. I could tell by his face he didn't want that. Was my book in English? Yes, I told him, my book is in English. He didn't want the Divine Liturgy celebrated in any other language than the one he, and the grey part of his parish, spoke as their primary language.

I ignored his attitude, and he didn't push the point any further. We celebrated the Liturgy, and I did all my parts in English. I think the priest was surprised the roof of the church did not cave in. But he was even more surprised when, at a dinner they had after the Liturgy, more than a few of his people approached me to thank me for using English. Some said to me it was the first time in the history of their (local) church that English had been used in the Divine Liturgy.

A couple of things made this experience unforgettable. The first was the attitude of the priest, who simply could not wrap his mind around the fact that some Orthodox priests did not speak or read his language. How isolated can some Orthodox Christians become? I would have understood his attitude if we were in the "old country," but we weren't. I should have asked him, "Have you noticed that everyone around you speaks English? Are they really undeserving of the gospel of Jesus Christ?" But I didn't think of it at the time.

The second thing that sticks in my memory was the piety of the people and their faithfulness. Many of the people in this church could not understand what words were being spoken during the Divine Liturgy, or even during the sermon. And yet they kept coming. Even the ones who spoke the modern version of the language could not understand the words of the Liturgy—even the Scripture readings. But the priest was correct—there were lots of people in church that day. There were many people who wanted to be there for the celebration of their church's name day.

How does it happen that hundreds of people show up to an event conducted in a language they don't understand?

Of course, we all know the family magnet is very powerful. Some of the people in the church that day had come for no spiritual reason whatsoever, but only because the feast day at the church had become a family tradition.

They came to keep Grandma or Grandpa happy. But that didn't account for everyone by any means. Many of the people genuinely loved God and wanted to worship God and grow in their faith. It was *difficult* for them, because of the language, but it was also *easy* for them because of the language. The language took them to a place where their family and people had been going for generations—a place of spirituality, comfort, familiarity, and unity. The literal meaning of the words neither contributed to nor detracted from that sensation. It had to do with the sound of the words, the place, the people, the smells, the cadence of the priest's voice, the music, and so on.

But Christianity is not a sensation. It is the truth that has established the universe. How can I believe in the truth—how can I have faith in the truth—when I don't understand it? When the words are clear, I can make the faith my own. But sometimes the words aren't very clear.

How about you? When you go to a Divine Liturgy and you can't understand some of the words, what do you do? Put your mind on hold and just stand there? Or think about other things? If you talk to someone, and you can't understand anything that person says, why would you keep going back to talk to them more? As St. Paul says, "What is *the conclusion* then? I will pray with the spirit, and I will also pray with the understanding. I will sing with the spirit, and I will also sing with the understanding" (1 Cor. 14:15).

I want to give you some ideas for what you can do to grow in your spiritual life, and in spiritual understanding, even in a parish where you can't understand all the words that are spoken or sung. It's worth the effort. Why? Because the priest stands between you and God, praying for you and bringing God's grace to you. Perhaps you don't understand every word he says while he's doing those things. But that doesn't mean they don't get said. When you stand in a room where miracles are taking place—the miracle of God's mercy, the miracle of His love, the miracle of the bread and wine becoming

His Body and Blood—your soul is enlightened. It's enlightened because there is a language of love and mercy that rises above the languages of men.

3. I Don't Know What's Going On

Our chanter was also our choir director. He was a fixture of the church—in my first several years at the parish, he never missed a Sunday. One day he told us he had to go to a wedding and would not be in church the following Sunday. I had the choir stay after so I could talk with them. Could they get through a Liturgy without him? "Sure," they all said. "No problem. We know what to do, Father! Don't worry!"

The following week, I started the Divine Liturgy. The choir was assembled, and they all had their books. I sang, "Blessed is the Kingdom of the Father, and of the Son, and of the Holy Spirit, now and ever, and unto ages of ages!"

Silence. I waited. More silence. I turned around and looked at the choir. They were all looking at me as if I were pointing a gun at them. Finally, one of them whimpered, "Amen?"

Okay, they just needed to get started, right? I turned back to the altar and sang, "In peace let us pray to the Lord."

Silence. I waited. More silence. I turned around and looked at the choir. They were all looking at me, again, as if I were pointing a gun at them. Finally, someone whimpered, "Lord have mercy?"

Oh my, was this going to be a long Liturgy.

After a little while, they started to get it. But I have to tell you about one more part. After the little entrance, when the choir sings the various troparia of the day, the woman who was "leading" at that point *actually chanted the words*, "Now sing the troparion of the church" (printed as a rubric in her choir book). On top of this, the choir members could not remember how to start the troparion of the church (the hymn of the parish's patron sung at every service), even though some of them had sung it literally hundreds of times before.

A couple of things still astonish me when I remember that Sunday. First, I still find it hard to believe these people couldn't sing a Liturgy on their own. Some of the choir members were quite old and had been in church nearly every Sunday of their lives. But they still needed a leader. When those choir members walked into the church, they switched their minds to low battery power. They turned the dimmer to "bovine." Do you know what I mean? Some folks walk into the church and stop thinking. There are times in our lives when we must be extremely alert, places we are expected to be the leaders who make critical decisions. For most people, church is not one of those times or places.

The choir members that day simply could not switch their minds over to full power. Singing in the choir had always been easy. Why, they may have wondered, wouldn't it continue to be easy? Answer: It's not going to be easy because the person who tells you exactly what to do and when to do it isn't here. So when they stood there bovining, the only thing that told them to sing was the long, deep silence and my irritated stare.

I know you're not like that. You are not a person who puts your mind into "bovine" when you walk into the church. Are you? Sure, you may rely on a leader—the priest, the chanters, or the choir director. You may not be able to walk in and start leading things by yourself. But simply because they're leading, does that make you a dull and unthinking follower?

Secondly, when the woman who had started "leading" the choir actually chanted the rubrics, it told me she had no idea what was actually happening during a Divine Liturgy. She might have been able to tell if I had done something differently than I had before, but she would only have known it was different because it sounded or looked funny to her, not because she knew what should be done. I used this opportunity to ask people in that parish about the Liturgy—why we do certain things certain ways. Almost none of them could answer my questions.

The most spectacular miracle in human history takes place every Sunday in your church—the miracle of the bread becoming the Body and the wine becoming the Blood of God. Every word of the Divine Liturgy prepares for that miracle, celebrates it, points to it, makes it possible, and describes it. It's a beautiful and awesome thing. If you don't know what's going on, you're missing something you definitely shouldn't be missing.

Find a liturgy book and follow along. Get to know the parts of the Divine Liturgy, what each means and how each part contributes to the whole. Imagine that a friend of yours came to church with you and afterward asked you what all of it meant. You don't want to simply say, "I don't know." That would be pathetic. Rather, imagine yourself explaining a couple of elements of the Liturgy to your friend in such a way that he decides he really wants to come and visit your church again.

4. I'm Being Forced to Go

When I was growing up, kids in my neighborhood would bowl in a Saturday morning league in the next town over. It was cheap and fun, and everyone did it. The mom who always drove us to the bowling alley also went to our church, off and on. She would often try to get me to talk her son into going to church. He didn't want to, and I didn't want to talk to him about it. My policy was, leave me out of it.

"Are we going to church tomorrow?" she would ask him in the car. He would roll his eyes. "David goes to church. You like church, don't you, David?"

"Yeah, I guess," I would say.

"Why don't you like church?" she would say to her son. He would roll his eyes again. "David, what fun things are they doing at church tomorrow?"

"I don't know," I would say.

This happened often. Fortunately, the ride was not long and we really enjoyed bowling.

One thing really surprised me about these neighbors, and it still surprises me when I see it in other families. My friend's mother should have *made* her son go to church. We were not that old! When I woke up on Sunday morning, my mother told me we were going to church, and discussion was not an option.

Why do parents refuse to accept their responsibility for their children's spiritual lives? I think it's mostly because they don't know why a person should go to church and they don't understand what goes on there. Of course, most adults have a vague sense that church is good for children and young people, and so they want the children to go, but they don't want to make the effort to go themselves. I had a family in a church one time where the man would drop the kids off at church and then go get coffee and bagels for himself and his wife. After the parents finished breakfast at home, they would come to church to visit their friends at the coffee hour and pick up the kids. Even as I write this now, I can't believe someone would do something like that.

But on the other hand, that basically describes the situation in my family growing up. My mother, as I said, always made me go to church. My father didn't go, and my mother didn't always go. But I had to go, even if I went by myself. It felt kind of funny to be known in the neighborhood as "the kid who goes to church," but really, it never occurred to me that I had a choice in the matter.

How about you? If you were forced to go to church as a child, or if you're being forced to go now, how can you make it into something you want to do? Part of you knows your parents wanted you to go to church because it made them look good. But they also wanted you to go to church because it's good to go to church. When your parents told you not to cross the street without looking both ways, did they do that so everyone would call them good parents? Not at all! They did it so you would keep living. It's the same thing with church—they knew it's a benefit to be in the church. Perhaps your parents didn't, or don't, quite know how to express that. But why don't you change that for yourself? Why don't you decide to get it right, so that as a parent, you know exactly what the benefit of church is?

If you were forced to go to church, you were given a blessing many kids in our world do not have. Make the most of that experience.

5. The Church Is Full of Hypocrites

When my wife and I attended our first Orthodox Divine Liturgy, the entire service was in a language we did not understand. I remember getting a little bored with the service until just after the people went forward for Holy Communion. Then it got interesting. As soon as everyone had taken communion, the priest yelled, "Get back in here! This is a holy day! You have time to stay until the end!" These were the first English words I had heard that morning.

My wife and I looked back at the doors of the church and saw most of the people there—they were crowded together in the narthex, trying to leave. They were all chatting with one another. At the priest's outburst, most of them fell silent and sheepishly made their way back to the pews.

The memory of this incident still shocks me. The priest and the people obviously assumed that no one except Orthodox Christians, and specifically their ethnic brand of Orthodox Christians, would be attending the Divine

Liturgy that day. If the priest had announced after reading the Gospel, "Just to let you know, we have visitors here today," do you think the same thing would have happened? I don't think so. Sure, some of the people would try to get away immediately after Communion. But others would want to stay—perhaps in order to show their best face, perhaps in order to meet the visitors.

But no. They thought they were "alone" and were clearly not on their best behavior. Isn't there something rather depressing about that? I realize, in one way of looking at it, that my wife and I were getting to see a family in a private moment. But that's the problem. Every Divine Liturgy has the potential to be like St. Innocent's Liturgy east of Sitka—a "spectacle" that leads someone to faith in Christ. What I saw was indeed a spectacle, but not in the good meaning of the term. There was a choir loft but no choir, no bulletin, no liturgy books in the pews, and frankly, the place needed to be cleaned.

And along with that, what was going on with that priest? He had obviously come to the point of losing his temper. As he distributed the Body and Blood of Christ to his people in Holy Communion, his anger grew and grew. He looked up now and then and saw them chatting, moving toward the exit, perhaps laughing at a funny remark. He'd had enough. *Why do I try to minister to these people Sunday after Sunday when it seems like they're never going to get it?* So, when his anger reached the boiling point, he yelled at them.

And the people? One could tell by the looks on their faces when the priest got angry that they knew exactly what they should have been doing. And they also knew they weren't doing it. They knew they should respect the church and the chalice. But they didn't want to. They hadn't seen their friends all week long and they wanted to tell them something, or just say hi. And of course, they had more important things to do than to stay in the church until the end of the Liturgy.

So why were these people doing what they were doing that day? Why did the priest celebrate that Divine Liturgy, and why did the people come? Force of habit, one would assume. An elderly woman in my church likes to joke, "I'm ninety-five years old. I've been dead for five years; I just don't have the good sense to lie down." Could it be that certain people that come to church have been *spiritually* dead for years, but they don't have the good sense to stay home?

No! Not at all. The beautiful thing about the Divine Liturgy is that it possesses a life and power of its own, irrespective of the celebrant or the people. We cannot decide there is no hope for someone just because, at the moment we see and judge, they appear to be faithless and distracted.

After all, if someone watched you every moment of your life, would he say, "Wow. That's the best Christian I've ever seen, a real asset to the Kingdom of God"? I can't answer for you, but I can say for myself there are many times in my life, many times each day, when you could rightfully judge me as anything but an "asset" to the Kingdom of God.

It's true that when you go to church on Sunday, you're going to see people who appear to be hypocrites. They come in late, leave early, and talk during the Divine Liturgy. When you see them, it's almost impossible not to judge them, because sometimes their behavior is truly deplorable. Sometimes they're rather blatant in their casual attitude. But you can decide right now, as you're reading this, *not* to judge them. You can decide to act as a force for good, praying for people rather than building grudges. Decide to be exactly the opposite of what you're judging them to be.

6. It's Just Not That Exciting

I knew someone who was a computer genius. He owned his own company, made lots of money, and did what he loved every day of the week. At least, it appeared that way on the surface. With all the money he made and all the work he got (because everyone wanted to hire him), he still held down a second job doing what he *really* loved.

On weekends several times a year, he would help a company install cell phone towers. His job was to climb up on the tower after everything was in place to attach all the cables and routers and fittings and so on. He got paid well, but he told me a number of times that he would do the job as a volunteer if they didn't pay him. Why? The thrill. He told me it was not uncommon for the wind to move the tower back and forth as much as ten feet while he was on it. When the company made him put on a safety harness, he would take it off after he started climbing. Often he would just go up without one. He was addicted to it. He told me he would stay at the top after he was done with the work in order to enjoy the rush of being hundreds of feet off the ground on a slender, waving aluminum frame.

A couple of things amazed me about this guy. I've already spoken to you about the woman working in the insurance agency and how she has arranged her life so that she is never bored at work. To some degree, my computer consultant had done the same thing; but rather than finding ways to make his average day more interesting, he added something to his life that he could look forward to.

But here's a problem: This man had a wife and two children. Not only did his second job keep him from his family during ten or so weekends each year, but he was also pointlessly toying with death. His mind—he was one of the smartest people I've ever met—caused him to be almost permanently dissatisfied with everything. He had few challenges he could not meet easily. In short, life bored him.

This cannot be the way it is with you. Yes, you're intelligent, more intelligent than most people. Yes, you work hard at what you do, and you're good at it. That much you share with my computer consultant. But listen. You have a challenge that will never allow you to live a dissatisfied, distracted, and bored life. That challenge is: Know God. Listen to what our Lord Jesus Christ said to God when He was praying for us: "And this is eternal life, that they may know You, the only true God, and Jesus Christ whom You have sent" (John 17:3). Do you want a thrill? Seek eternal life. It's a delightful challenge that virtually never gets boring.

Be filled with the Holy Spirit. Make yourself into a vessel that is perfect to contain the Holy Spirit, in the same way a bucket is perfect for carrying water. This is a task with which you will never grow bored.

The second thing that made me sad about my friend the computer consultant was his attitude about the purpose of life. For certain people, the time they have in this world serves only themselves, as if they own the time of their lives like a commodity. And since they own it, they spend it on themselves: on their comfort, on thrills, on things that make them feel good about themselves. This man had gone to school for sixteen years, then graduated, got married, bought a house, and started a family. His company was prospering. The only goal he hadn't reached when I knew him was retirement. Is that really all there is to life? Birth, school, job, marry, family, retire, death. My consultant saw himself as drawing close to the step before death, and it made him unhappy. No wonder people spend so much time trying to find distractions!

Now certainly, we do well to pursue these things, like getting an education and having a family. But do they, in themselves, comprise a purpose of life? Not at all! God has given you the time that comprises your life. It's a gift. God wants you to know Him and to seek eternal life. He wants you to be full of Himself, to be a vessel for the Holy Spirit. When you make it your goal in life to seek the things of this world, and nothing more, then boredom is inevitable.

When you're in church and you feel like you're bored, ask yourself, Where else am I going to seek and find the purpose of my life? At a party, in front of a TV, hanging around with my friends? In a class at school? Those places are important, or fun, as far as that goes. But they're not going to give you a purpose for your life. Not the way attending to the Divine Liturgy will.

THOSE ARE MY SIX REASONS people often find church boring. I bet you could come up with a few more. Now, what do we do about it? How do we make it so that we have more than these two options: (1) be bored in church, or (2) don't go? Before we answer this question, we have a few more stops to make.

Chapter Seven

Five Ways of Looking at Your Priest

WE'VE TALKED ABOUT SIX REASONS church could be called "boring." Do you agree with me that every one of those things really has more to do with *you*, and your attitude, than with the church? Well, there's more. My six reasons had to do with your attitude toward the Liturgy, but your attitude about something else—or I should say some*one* else—will also determine the extent to which you think church is boring.

I'm talking about the priest. No matter who your priest is, how he celebrates the Liturgy, how he preaches, or what language he speaks, you can still change your attitude toward the church by viewing his role differently. (I don't mean "role" in the sense of a role played by an actor, but in the sense of "function.")

Role One: Lawyer

Imagine you break the law and get arrested. It's a very serious situation, so what do you do? You get a lawyer.

This is not unlike what happens in the Christian life. You regularly break God's law, so the best thing to do is to enlist the help of an intermediary to plead your case before the court. Of course, your real lawyer is our Lord

Jesus Christ: "And if anyone sins, we have an Advocate with the Father, Jesus Christ the righteous" (1 John 2:1). But who advocates for you before Christ? Who prays for you and leads you in prayer? Your priest.

But let's go back to the secular illustration. What do you do when you get a lawyer? You pay him money (lots of it), tell him what you did, and then—what? You sit back, and he does the work. Suppose research needs to be done—who does it? Suppose a motion needs to be filed—who does it? And if the prosecutor calls, whom does he ask for? The lawyer. He does everything. You just wait and hope. And pay.

For some people, this is the perfect image of the priest. These are the people who do not want to go to hell when they die, but they don't want to do anything spiritual in this life. So what can they do? Give money to the Church, and then expect the priest to take care of everything. These people want zero responsibility.

Is that your attitude? If so, I feel sorry for you. You're missing the joy and satisfaction of the spiritual life. It's like paying someone to go to the movies for you or to go on a vacation for you. Someone is enjoying himself, but it's sure not you.

There is another pitfall as well. The people who pay their priest to get them to heaven think of their priest as nothing but a hired hand, an employee. Therefore, they are always judging him. When you have employees, you have to critique their job performance. Certain people do this with the priest.

Imagine you've hired a lawyer to get you off the hook for a crime you've committed. You know you're guilty, but you don't want to go to jail. The lawyer takes your case and your money and starts doing things, most of which you don't understand. The trial gets closer and closer, and you start to worry. You call the lawyer's office and the secretary tells you he's golfing.

Golfing! He should be working 24/7 on my case. If he loses my case, I'll show him how to use a golf club! What am I paying him for? You're angry because, in your opinion, he's not doing his job.

Then when he shows up to the trial, imagine he's wearing a tie he got— where? Disneyland? Did his kid make that for him? How dare he dress like that for this trial! You're disappointed and angry again, because you've decided he can't possibly be a good lawyer. He just doesn't look the part.

And then the jury comes out of the room and gives their decision. You've been found—what? If we're talking about the priest, and you're paying him to keep you out of hell after you die, you're not going to know the outcome until it's too late. Too late to get your money back.

Is that your attitude? Heavens, no! When you come to church, do not put your priest in the role of a lawyer. He doesn't want that, and neither do you.

Role Two: Doctor

You wake up one morning in extreme pain. Who do you call? Your doctor. You need to find someone with the expertise to diagnose and treat whatever it is that you have. Someone with a license to prescribe medications.

Later in the day, if you're lucky, you go to the doctor's office. After waiting long past the time of your appointment, you go in. The doctor examines you and then tells you what you need to do. Keep something elevated. Drink lots of water. Go get some medicine. Soak something in something. Exercise more.

Are you going to do those things? Some people do exactly what the doctor says. Others do part of what the doctor says. Many people don't do anything at all, except maybe take a pill. The do-nothing group thinks of the doctor as a lawyer—he's expected to do it all, and they don't do anything.

But that's not the way it is with doctors. They have the expertise, they do some things for you without your help, and they collect data that helps them figure out what's wrong. But they cannot work alone. They need your participation.

For some people, this is the perfect image of the priest. We are, all of us, sick with a disease—sin. The priest has the expertise to provide the right treatment for the disease, but he needs your help. Things will go much better for you if you do some of the work yourself. He can prescribe medications, but you have to go get them yourself, and then take them. He can tell you what to eat, for instance, but he's not going to come to your house every day and feed you like a baby.

Is that your attitude? Do you see your priest as a kind of physician? If so, you're on the right track. Someone much smarter than I said, "Firstly, I must underline that the Church is a spiritual hospital which heals man."[10] Also, "The fact that Christianity is considered and called a therapeutic treatment . . . reveals that clergymen—who are not simply the representative of Christ on earth, but the mystery of the true presence of Christ—are, of course, also therapists of the people of God."[11]

But if you're on the right track, and you can see your priest as a "therapist of the people of God," you also have to know that you have responsibility for your own spiritual life. You can't just come to church every now and then and hope to be cured. That's like saying, "If I go and stand in a hospital lobby for an hour or so each week, I'll be healthy." No, your physical health depends on what you eat, how you exercise, your state of mind. These things result from your decisions and your follow-through. It's the same with your

---

10   Met. Hierotheos Vlachos, *The Illness and Cure of the Soul in the Orthodox Tradition*, trans. Mavromichali (Levadia, Greece: Birth of the Theotokos Monastery, 1993), p. 81.

11   *Op. cit.*, p. 91.

spirit. When you make good decisions and follow through on them, you have a healthy spirit.

Without that, when you visit the physician of souls, he might have nothing to say except, "There's nothing more I can do. Just go home and try to remain comfortable."

Role Three: Teacher

Everyone reading this has had a teacher. Some teachers are exciting and inspirational, and some are not. But no matter what kind of teacher you have, there is one important element they all share: The reason you have a relationship with any teacher is that you want to learn something. Or, perhaps more often, someone else wants you to learn something. When I worked in health care, I would have to go to seminars to keep my license current. I often did not want the information I was getting at these seminars, but I had to go to keep my job. I really disliked these required seminars, because I almost never learned anything.

I want you to ask yourself: If my priest is a kind of teacher, what am I learning? And I don't mean things like what the colors in the icons mean or what year the first ecumenical council took place. I mean, how are you changing as a result of your relationship with the Church? If you took a "spirit" test at church each year, would it show a progression, year to year, of some kind? A development of the spirit? Or would it just show that your body was in the building every now and then, with no discernible impact?

Look at your priest as a teacher. He has something to teach you. Don't regard church as a seminar you have to sit through. The Church has something to teach you. What is it? It's how to be a human being. How to be a Christian. It's not as easy as it sounds, and the more you learn, the more you find you don't know.

"Show me Your ways, O LORD; / Teach me Your paths. / Lead me in Your truth and teach me, / For You *are* the God of my salvation; / On You I wait all the day" (Psalm 25:4–5).

Role Four: Artist

What do artists do in our society? They express our sense of ourselves. The art that touches you—music, visual art, writing—does so because you feel understood. Different kinds of people like different kinds of art, or music, or books. Why does that happen? It happens because the art must express different things to reach its audience. Even this book you're holding right now— you're reading it because, to some degree, you identified with the title.

Art lets you express your sense of yourself, but good art takes you a step further. Good art does more than make you feel understood; it also challenges you to expand your vision of the world. When I hear a moving song about unrequited love, I feel my own experiences of unrequited love. But when the song is really good, I additionally feel sympathy for the artist, a connection to someone outside myself. I feel a link to anyone who has experienced unrequited love, and this makes me a better person. It helps me grow.

The Divine Liturgy, the music, the icons, the vestments, the building— all these aspects of the Church—are artistic. Of course, their primary purpose is to communicate the glory of God and to lead us to repentance, so their artistic quality is not the same as that of other works of art. If I'm playing a video game and I'm amazed at the quality of the graphics, it's not the same thing as seeing an icon and knowing that it is also a beautiful work of art.

In addition to this, your priest is an artist. He sings, he creates sermons, he leads you in worship. Do you agree? It may be difficult to see your priest as an artist, but it's necessary if you want the Divine Liturgy to take you

beyond a simple sense of ethnic or religious identification. Yes, you're Orthodox, and attending the Divine Liturgy is what Orthodox people do. But when
you see the priest as an artist who is challenging you to move beyond that,
beyond simply standing there because that's what Orthodox people do, then
you open yourself to be filled by the Holy Spirit. You give yourself the opportunity to become aflame with the love of God.

Role Five: Manager

Next time you walk into a store, look around as if you were the store manager. Is it clean? Are all the employees where they should be? Do all the lights
work properly? Are the shelves fully stocked?

Looking at a store, a hospital, a school, with the eyes of a manager gives
you a very different perspective on things. The manager is the person you
probably don't see, but he's responsible for everything that takes place in
his building, department, or institution. When I was the administrator of a
large health care facility, the success I enjoyed came from one thing: I always
had the attitude that everything that happened in that facility was my direct
responsibility. Of course, I had a staff who actually did the work, and I'm not
a nurse or an accountant. But every moment of every day, I walked through
the building, saying, "Everything I see, good or bad, is my responsibility." In
my opinion, that's part of what a good manager does.

Some people see the Church as an institution and the priest as the manager of that institution. This is correct only to a degree. The Church is the
living Body of Christ: "Now you are the body of Christ, and members indi-
vidually" (1 Cor. 12:27). It is a human association, but it is also a divine body
through which God imparts His mercy to the world. We can compare it to
other human institutions as a point of discussion, but the Church is entirely
different from all other human institutions.

So, to see the Church as an institution and the priest as a manager has its limits. Those who see the Church *only* as an institution find themselves looking for the places where the manager has fallen short: the cleanliness of the building, the quality of the newsletter/bulletin, or the relevance of the programming.

Every church has people like this. A man approached me in a church where I was pastor and said, "Father, the bulb in the spotlight for the sign is burnt out." I could tell that, by giving me this information, he felt like he had done his good deed for the day.

"Oh," I said. "Where are the bulbs kept?"

"They're in a drawer in the kitchen, Father. The one on the right, just inside the doorway."

"Okay, then. Go to that drawer, get a bulb, and fix the spotlight."

He did it, but I could tell that he really didn't think it was his job to change light bulbs.

Certainly, that's one way of seeing the priest as a manager. It's similar to the priest as lawyer—he gets paid, so he should take care of everything.

But there is another way to look at the priest as manager. If he's the manager, who is his staff? In the parish in the example above, I was. I was the custodian, the secretary, the treasurer, and also the priest. I used to say to the parish council, "If something doesn't get done, I go into the bathroom and give the guy in the mirror a good talking-to." But this is not the way it should be.

Who is the priest's staff? You are! Let's think for a moment: What would you do if you drove up to the church and noticed a light bulb was burnt out?

1.   You *wouldn't* notice it. You don't notice anything about the church.

2.   You could ignore it.

3.   You could say to yourself, "It figures. This place always looks crummy."

4.   You could say the same thing to a friend.

5.   You could tell the priest he should fix it.

6.   Or here's another idea. You could ask the priest if it's okay for you to change the bulb, and if he says it is, then fix it yourself. This is how you make the church your own.

Chapter Eight

Four Ways of Serving the Church

LET'S BUILD ON THE IDEA that you should make the church your own. The priest (and by extension, the bishop) is your manager who also happens to be a physician, an artist, and a teacher. You come to the church as part of his staff. You come to work. Church time is not grazing time; it's time for you to take responsibility. If everyone in the church were the kind of parishioner you are, would they have to build an addition or close the doors for good? Ask yourself that question every now and then—it will help you make the church your own.

Remember, my beloved, that there are limits to your "ownership" of the church. I cannot count the number of times people have come to me with requests that I cannot agree to because they are contrary to the teachings of the Church. Most of the time people make those kinds of requests because they believe they are more special than anyone else and the church should conform to their specialness. No. I want you to make the church your own as a servant, not as a master. We have a master already, our bishop. Unless you're a bishop, you must express your "ownership" of the church only through servanthood.

But as servants, there is much we can do. What? *Anything*, that's what!

When our children were young, we would take vacations that were designed for them. Amusement parks and things like that. As they got older, we often went camping—but a problem began to develop. My wife and I would go camping to relax, sit, and go on little hikes to look at things. The kids were bored. They wanted to *do* something. So one summer, I took the family to the High Peaks region of New York, and we climbed a mountain. When we got to the top, I said, "That's number one. There are forty-five more high peaks in the Adirondacks, and people consider it a great accomplishment to climb them all. Do we, as a family, want to give it a try?" Everyone got excited about the project, and we were off and climbing. We've done twenty so far.

So family vacations were back in style. We often camp while we're in the High Peaks, and while my wife and I have a great time relaxing, we also schedule time to climb huge mountains. It's a real challenge, but also fun. It's almost like we have a collection of mountains, and each summer we add one or two to our collection. Plus, we've had some adventures. Once we got lost in the forest and it started raining like the end of the world. Now that's good family fun for you! And why? Because we had *something to do*.

I'm convinced this is where the practice of having children serve in the altar comes from. It gives them something to do. I love children. I love spending time with children. There is really only one time when I do not particularly want to spend time with children—and it's the time when I'm most surrounded by children. Sundays during the Liturgy!

But you know what? I'll put up with a little (a *little*) fidgeting during the Liturgy if it gets families to come to church. And helping in the altar is just one place you can find something to do. Let's look at four of them.

One: Singer

Isn't music one of the most important parts of our worship? Really, of our lives?

Sometimes the choir and the chanters in a church seem a little intimidating to outsiders. A little like a closed society. You know what you should do? Kick in the door to the closed society and become a part of it. If you have a good voice at all, you should consider doing this. You'll be surprised that, most of the time, the choir and the chanters love having a younger person (with some choirs, that's anyone under sixty) express interest. They want to pass on their art to the next generation.

Or if the choir's not for you, learn to chant, if your church has chanters. It's easy joining the chanters. Oftentimes, anyone who wants to learn chanting simply goes up and stands at the chanter's stand while the regular chanters chant. That's the best way to learn—listen. Look at the books they use and where they keep those books. Watch them get ready to chant. Talk to them. You may be there a long time before you begin to contribute in any beautiful way, but it's the best place to start. Also, there are many online resources; find out which ones the chanters at your parish use the most.

Let me say one word about church choirs: beware. My experience has been that some church choirs have an "off the clock" attitude. I mean they pay attention to the Liturgy when they're singing, but as soon as they stop singing, they stop paying attention. They chat. They arrange their music. They sell tickets to dances and raffles. They wander around. In some parishes, the choir sings up at the front of the church, so this "off the clock" attitude is minimized somewhat. But when the choir is in the back of the church or on a balcony, it's very difficult for the choir members to feel themselves a part of the Liturgy unless they're actually singing.

Here's an idea: Join the choir and show them what it's like when choir members love every single word, every single minute, of the Divine Liturgy.

Two: Reader

I think this is a much more important position than people realize. People love to hear their children read, but mostly it's because they want to see their kid do something in church and they don't really mind if they can't understand a word he says. That's too bad. The person who reads should read loud and clear, and in a way that emphasizes (to a reasonable degree) the meaning of the words.

This means that serving as a reader takes two things: a strong voice and a little preparation. It's easy to simply walk into the church and read the epistle. Sure, maybe the person who prepares a little doesn't read any differently. But each word is important. Each word teaches the people about the spiritual life, about God's love, about repentance and forgiveness. These are important things to know, and the reader has the responsibility of conveying those words clearly.

I don't only mean that you should know how to pronounce "Melchisedek." I mean that when St. Paul writes, "I have been crucified with Christ, it is no longer I who live, but Christ lives in me," the words should ring through the church like a clear and lovely bell and fill the hearts of the people.

Three: Priest's Helper

Altar servers! I've got a million stories about altar servers. I had one altar server who set himself on fire. (Just his hair. I learned that day that burning hair really smells terrible. Not a good substitute for incense.) I've had some who were continually knocking things over, others who could not stand still and stop talking. A couple of them gobbled all the antidoron during the Liturgy so there was almost none for the people at the end.

But I've also had altar servers who were so good, they almost seemed like an extension of my mind. One of my altar servers, the best I ever had, never needed me to say a word or make any signs with my hands. I would simply look at him and he would know what I needed. I never heard him speak behind the altar. This is the kind of altar server that makes our worship beautiful. The other kind makes their parents and grandparents proud, but they are sometimes a burden to the priest and a distraction to the community.

But not you! If you are male, I want you to start serving in the altar in a way that contributes to the worship of the faithful. Make it so that the priest is glad to see you, not simply because you're in church, but because he knows having you behind the altar will make that Divine Liturgy a spiritual joy for him and for his parishioners.

I have a question about altar servers: Why do they have to be children? I had a very good altar server one time who was a real help to me. When he started going to college, he stopped serving in the altar. I asked him why. He told me everyone did it that way, that it would be considerate of him to step aside and let the younger guys learn how to take over in the altar. No matter how much I asked him to reconsider, I could see he felt helping as an altar server was something only kids did.

Don't you do that! I don't care how old you are—if God is calling you to serve in the altar and the priest needs you, don't lose the opportunity by worrying about what other people think.

Four: Intercessor

Perhaps you've read this chapter so far and you don't want to do any of these things. You're not going to sing, you're not going to read, and you can't serve in the altar because you're female. So does that mean you have nothing to do during the Liturgy? Not at all.

You can accept the most important mission of all.

Next time you go to church, look around you. There are people there who need your prayers. Pray for them. Become an intercessor. Don't judge them! That's not the task of an intercessor. The task of an intercessor is to pray for people. Perhaps there are things you can pray for that you know about, but remember there are many more things you don't know about. You might not even know someone's name. You can still pray for that person.

My first parish was very small. It was so small that sometimes I didn't have anything to do. I'm a jittery person, and I get unhappy when I don't have anything to do. While my kids were in school and my wife was at work, I would sometimes go to the church, stand or sit outside on the lawn, and pray for all the cars that went by. Not the cars, the people in the cars. I would bless them as they drove down our road. Did that help? Yes, it most certainly did!

There is never a time when we pray for people, even people we don't know, that it does not help them in some way. How many times did the cars stop, the people get out, walk over to me, and say, "Hey, thanks for praying for me. I want to convert to Orthodoxy and come to your church and donate large amounts of money and time." Never! Remember, the task of an intercessor is to pray for people, not to wonder if your specific prayer has helped a specific person. I'll tell you now—it does. Don't worry about it. It does.

But remember, an intercessor does not ignore the Divine Liturgy in order to pray for people. You have to remember why you're in church—to worship God—and approach that task diligently. However, when your mind starts to wander, your feet start to hurt, and you're getting fidgety to be someplace else, that's a good time to pray. I love this passage from one of St. Gregory Palamas's sermons: "Come then, holy company, hallowed audience, choir in harmony with the Holy Spirit, and assist me with this address, making it a joint effort, not just by listening attentively and directing your thoughts, but also by providing help through your sincere prayers, that the Word of the Father may join in from heaven with my words about His Mother."[12] St. Gregory asked his people to pray for him as he preached. You should do that too—pray for the priest during the Divine Liturgy and during the sermon.

Let yourself be filled with the Holy Spirit, and listen to who or what He is asking you to pray for.

The Next Step

Back in chapter one, we looked at what it means to be bored. Boredom is a feeling, and often you can change your feelings by changing your mind. It doesn't always work that way, but it certainly does in relation to feeling bored in church.

So really, everything I say pertains to the battle for the mind. I've suggested ways you can keep your mind occupied in church by doing things like chanting or reading. But really, that only addresses the symptoms, not the root problem. The root problem of a wandering mind is not solved simply by finding something to do. If your mind is wandering, eventually it will find someplace else it wants to be and make you feel bad because you're not there. You can be just as bored while you're helping in the altar as you can be outside the altar, even though you get to pick up a candle and walk around a couple of times. You can be bored doing anything, and having something to occupy your mind helps only to a degree.

The fact is that distracting yourself so you don't get bored will never provide a long-term substitute for the genuine, heartfelt, all-consuming worship of God. To achieve this, you need to bring your mind under control. Or, at least, *more* under control. Think of it as a continuum: on one end you

---

12   St. Gregory Palamas, *The Homilies*, trans. Christopher Veniamin (Waymart, PA: Mount Thabor Publishing, 2009), p. 416.

have twenty thoughts galloping around your head like a herd of puppies, and on the other end you have a mind as focused and attentive as an experienced seeing-eye dog. Try to move yourself a little more toward having some control over your thoughts. Perhaps you're not going to achieve guide-dog concentration at first, but you might be able to teach a puppy or two to stop pooping in the house.

Think about where your eyes go during the Divine Liturgy. Practice this: Look at one particular icon for as long as possible. Look at every aspect of the icon, the colors, the clothing, and the face. Don't think about the saint, just the icon. The icon is a passageway leading to another world, the heavenly Kingdom. Use the icon to go there. Use the Liturgy to go there. Allow every artistic element of that icon to fill your soul with the presence and love of God.

If you're serving in the altar, keep your eyes on the altar table. If you were a monk, I might say, "As soon as the gong has sounded leave the cell, your physical eyes downcast and your thought plunged deeply into the remembrance of God."[13] You're not a monk, but the advice is still good.

Or get a Liturgy book and follow along. For many years, I was against this; I didn't like having Liturgy books in the church for people to use. I thought it was a distraction. But one of my parishioners told me she always followed the book because it helped keep her mind on the Liturgy and away from her problems. She told me every week she would look at the words of the Liturgy and see something new. Sounds good to me! Now I always make sure the Liturgy book I'm using is the one available to the people as a tool in the fight against distraction.

Sometimes I try to stand perfectly still for a certain period of time during

---

13   Kadloubovsky and Palmer, trans., *Writings from the Philokalia on Prayer of the Heart* (London: Faber and Faber, 1951), p. 393.

long services. I try to become acutely aware of my body as a presence in the church building, as a part of the building—a piece of furniture or a part of the construction. I want to make myself as present in the Liturgy as possible. Yes, it isn't long before my mind starts to wander around, but when I'm completely focused on my body—stillness, breathing, guarding my eyes—then it cannot wander far. My mind becomes like a kid hooked to one of those kid leashes. It's forced to remain close by.

As we go on to the next chapter, we're going to move away from the idea that we should keep ourselves busy as a way of enjoying church more. We're stepping up a little higher. We're going to address ways of praying. This means the techniques like singing in the choir, focusing on our breathing, or following along with a Liturgy book will fall away. They are good ideas, but they are the lower steps. Get ready to move to a more mature level of spirituality and of being in the Divine Liturgy.

Chapter Nine

Three Kinds of Waiting

ANY WAY YOU CUT IT, there are going to be times when church drags a little. There are going to be times when you're simply waiting until the next thing happens. These are the times when your mind tends to drop into low gear. I call it "bovining." You try to force yourself to pray or to pay attention, but to no avail. What do you do then?

Well, you wait. Waiting is fine. But there are ways to wait that are helpful and ways that are not helpful at all. The way to make the services of the Church spiritually beneficial to you is to *wait in the right way*.

One Way of Waiting: Stoplight

Imagine you're driving somewhere, and you come to a red light. You stop the car, and what do you do? If you're an intelligent and peaceful person, you wait for the light to turn green. I say "intelligent and peaceful" because I find myself occasionally sitting in my car at a light behind people who cannot sit still; they apparently always have to be doing something. When this kind of person comes to a red light, she or he immediately begins to talk on the phone, text, read something, clean the car, adjust makeup, play with the car stereo, eat, drink, smoke, adjust the car seats of the children in the back, play with the dog—you know how it goes. Then when the light turns green, you have to beep your horn at them to get going.

But that's not you. When you come to a red light, you wait for the light to turn green. This is the first kind of waiting. It consists of just sitting there.

Some people attend church in this way. They vacate their minds as if they were waiting at a stoplight. They stop until they can go again. There are a couple of things wrong with this kind of waiting.

First, anything is better than going somewhere to do nothing but stop-light waiting. Since this kind of waiting is really nothing at all, these folks believe anything else that might come up on a Sunday morning is better than going to church. People complain to me sometimes that their children have sports on Sunday mornings. Why are they complaining to me? They know I have one response to their complaint, and it's this: "It's pathetic that you would put your children's souls in peril in order to have them play sports." Why do I say that? It's not only the particular Sundays the children are told they can miss, it's the idea that if something interesting comes along on a particular Sunday morning, church is the last on the list of places you want to be.

And yet this attitude makes sense if going to church is simply a matter of waiting until the light turns green so you can get on with life.

The second problem with stoplight waiting is that people who practice it don't know what's going on. Beautiful and profound things might be hap-pening virtually in front of their faces, and they miss them. These folks fall into a bovine stupor during church, and nothing short of an explosion can shake them out of it. I can see this when I'm preaching (of course, that's when I'm facing the people for an extended period of time). I might make an obscure reference in my sermon, or perhaps a pun, or something like that.

Many people, those who are listening, will catch the reference and react in some way. But the bovines sit, looking like they're grazing. Most people belong to a parish, but some folks belong to a herd. It's very frustrating.

This is not you. You are not bovine and never will be—the words "bovine stupor" will never describe you. Your mind is sharp and your eyes bright. You see what's happening during the Divine Liturgy. Perhaps it's something you don't understand, perhaps it's something you need to ask the priest about later. But you notice. This is good—it means when you're in church, you're not doing the same kind of waiting you do at a stoplight.

But what other options are there?

Another Way of Waiting: Christmas

All of us can remember as a child the days leading up to Christmas. I remember being so excited that I would lie on the floor on my side, make a running motion with my legs, and flop around in little circles. My dog would jump up and down and bark at me, then my mother would throw us both out into the snow. This would happen several times a day in the days leading up to Christmas.

At night, as I lay in bed before sleep, I would imagine what it was going to be like on Christmas morning. I would imagine the most unlikely and spectacular gifts: a live monkey, my own RV to live in, a jeep with a machine gun mounted on the back (my favorite TV program was *The Rat Patrol*). Of course, I never got any of those things. But that never stopped me from dreaming big.

This kind of waiting is different from stoplight waiting, because so much of it involves thinking ahead to what's coming. When you're at a stoplight, you don't say to yourself, "Oh, it's going to be the greatest day of my life when the light turns green and I can finally get going again!" But before Christmas, you may very well say, "When Christmas comes and I get the presents I expect, it will be the best day ever!"

Of course, "Christmas" waiting in church doesn't have the same kind of excitement that Christmas morning does. The people in church aren't thinking longingly about what comes next in the Divine Liturgy. Not at all. They don't say, "Oh, when these Psalms are finally done, it will be time for the Great Ektenia. That will be so great!" No. They say, "When church *is over* today, I'm going to have a really good lunch, or take a nap, or go to the movies, or play video games until my thumbs turn to bloody stumps." They think about what's coming *after church*. It's like church is December 24, and when it's over, that's Christmas.

There are a couple of things wrong with this kind of waiting. First, the Divine Liturgy is the place where we worship God. If we're spending the whole time thinking about what we want to do when it's over, then we never actually do what we're there to do.

Have you ever been speaking with someone who doesn't look at you, but instead constantly looks around to see who else they could talk to? I was recently at a reunion of people I hadn't seen for thirty years. The first person I spoke to did that over-the-shoulder scouting while he and I were catching up. He wanted to see if a more interesting person was attending the reunion. I launched a preemptive strike: as he was talking to me, and still not looking at me, I just walked away. After all, he didn't really want to talk to me, so why should I continue to put him through the misery? I guess that wasn't very nice, and I'm sorry now that I did it.

What if you had the chance to talk with a famous person? Or you were talking with the person you love more than anyone else in this world? Would your eyes wander around, looking for someone better? Of course not! And yet in our minds, we do this in church when we engage in Christmas waiting. We come to spend time with God, and the whole time we're thinking about more interesting places to be. That's not something you want to do. Insulting God the way my former high school "friend" insulted me is a bad idea.

The second problem with Christmas waiting in church is that once your mind wanders to a place where it wants to be outside the church, it's almost impossible to bring it back. It's like a teacher trying to teach a class of children on the day before Christmas break. No one can concentrate on anything.

Something like this happened to me the other day. Sometimes I take my dogs for an off-leash walk. We hike through the woods near my home, and I let them run. Usually, they're well behaved—unless they find something they like better than listening to me. Last week they found a dead deer. They didn't try to eat it, but they were so fascinated they would not come to me, no matter how much I called. I used my angry voice, and they ran a few steps toward me, then turned around and went back to the deer. It was too much to resist.

So it is with your mind. While you stand in church, your mind looks around for a dead deer to sniff, and when it finds one, you can't get it to come back into the church. Someone much wiser than I says it better: "Just as a man blind from birth does not see the sun's light, so one who fails to pursue watchfulness does not see the rich radiance of divine grace. He cannot free himself from evil thoughts, words and actions."[14]

Christmas waiting is not what you want to do in church; it's really almost as bad as stoplight waiting. But what other choice do you have?

---

14   Palmer, Sherrard, and Ware, trans., *The Philokalia: The Complete Text*, vol. 1 (London: Faber and Faber, 1979), p. 163.

The Best Way of Waiting: Restaurant

When I was very young, my extended family would get together at a nice restaurant in the city where my grandmother lived to celebrate big occasions. This was a nice place. The waiter would approach the table and just stand there, waiting for you to tell him what to do. He didn't introduce himself. He didn't rattle off a list of specials. He didn't suggest you order drinks first. He just stood there. And at the end of the meal, he didn't sneak up and try to take your plate while saying, "Are you still working on that?"

It was an expensive place, but I remember my father always said he liked to go there because they had real waiters. They never wrote anything down, and it always seemed like at the moment you needed them, they would see you and approach the table. And I literally never heard them speak. They must have, because I'm sure some customers had questions, but the impression made on me as a little boy was that this is the restaurant with the waiters who never talk.

This perfectly illustrates the third kind of waiting. How can a waiter memorize, on the spot, every detail of every order for ten or twelve people? The answer is easy: He pays attention. He's not thinking about anything except making sure you have the best experience possible at the restaurant where he works. His attention is on you, not on his girlfriend, not on what he's going to do when his shift is over, not on how much he wants to tell you that his feet hurt. My father had it right. These were real waiters.

There is a word for this in the Scriptures: *nepsis*. It means "watchfulness" or "attentiveness." It means you're waiting like a real waiter. I think nepsis is what our Lord had in mind when He said, "Blessed *are* the pure in heart, for they shall see God" (Matt. 5:8). What does it mean to be pure? Pure water, for instance, is only water and nothing else. The pure in heart focus on one thing; they do not allow the heart to wander around aimlessly. Like pure water, the pure heart does not have chunks of other things floating around in it.

How can we practice nepsis in church? The answer is easy: Guard the eyes, guard the mouth, guard the thoughts. But it's not easy to do: "Watchfulness is to be bought only at a great price."[15] If you decide to take my advice and guard the triple gateway to the heart (eyes, mouth, mind), you will find very quickly that this is a difficult task. Sometimes I even find myself concentrating so much on guarding my mind that thoughts *about* guarding my mind keep my mind away from the worship of God. Tell me that's not twisted. And yet these are the kinds of games your mind will play with you when you become serious about nepsis.

The key, I think, is practice. As with anything, you get better with practice. Think of the Divine Liturgy as a nepsis marathon. Or perhaps that's too much—more like a nepsis 5K. What would happen to you if you never ran at all and then just went and ran a 5K? One of my children tried that. I was running a 5K and he ran with me—but he didn't prepare at all. We finished the race, but I'll tell you, at the end he was hurting physically and in a terrible mood. It would have been much better if he had prepared a little; then we could have enjoyed the experience rather than endured it.

This is what I want for you. I want you to enjoy the Divine Liturgy, not endure it. When you learn to be a real waiter during the Liturgy—keeping your eyes on the table, keeping your selfish thoughts to a minimum, and not indulging in idle talk—you'll find a genuine joy that you hadn't known was there. Waves of love and mercy will wash over you, flowing from the altar. The Body and Blood of Christ will make your mouth into a gateway of the Divine, filling you with the very presence of God.

---

15 *Philokalia*, *op. cit.*, p. 162. This whole passage—and in fact, the whole section of the Philokalia attributed to St. Hesychios the Priest— is certainly worth your time if you're serious about nepsis.

Our Lord Talks about Nepsis

There is a great passage from Luke in which our Lord speaks to this issue of being a good waiter:

> Let your waist be girded and your lamps burning; and you your-selves be like men who wait for their master, when he will return from the wedding, that when he comes and knocks they may open to him immediately. Blessed *are* those servants whom the master, when he comes, will find watching. Assuredly, I say to you that he will gird himself and have them sit down *to eat*, and will come and serve them. And if he should come in the second watch, or come in the third watch, and find *them* so, blessed are those servants. But know this, that if the master of the house had known what hour the thief would come, he would have watched and not allowed his house to be broken into. Therefore you also be ready, for the Son of Man is coming at an hour you do not expect. (Luke 12:35–40)

In this passage, is our Lord giving us advice about how we can keep our houses safe? Not a chance. He's talking about your soul. There are forces that want to destroy your soul; they sneak up on you when you're not look-ing and wreak havoc.

I did a funeral once for a young man who died of a drug overdose. He had been involved with the church as a child but then fell away. He made friends with people who used drugs, and soon he was using drugs as well. Then he overdosed and died. Do you think his soul rose to paradise to dwell eternally with God? I'm not going to venture a guess. I would be glad if it did, but I also have to say I would not be surprised if it didn't.

When I read Luke 12:35–40, I don't think Jesus is saying, "If you get caught in a sin that destroys you, that's okay, you'll be fine in the afterlife."

Not at all. I think He was saying, "If your waist is not girded and your lamp is not burning, you run the risk of being caught off guard at the worst possible time, and you will lose your soul." In another place, our Lord says, "But take heed to yourselves, lest your hearts be weighed down with carousing, drunkenness, and cares of this life, and that Day come on you unexpectedly" (Luke 21:34).

In this light, you can see how nepsis is not optional. Nepsis is not something you try for awhile to see if you like it or not. Nepsis is like a strong stone wall built around a city so foreign armies will not be able to destroy it. Nepsis is the task of someone who constantly seeks wisdom: "Blessed is the man who listens to me, / Watching daily at my gates, / Waiting at the posts of my doors" (Prov. 8:34). Nepsis is like an athlete who is always practicing and training so he's prepared to do his best. Nepsis is spiritual survival in an unfamiliar and dangerous place.

St. Mark's Gospel also addresses the issue of nepsis:

"Take heed, watch and pray; for you do not know when the time is. *It is* like a man going to a far country, who left his house and gave authority to his servants, and to each his work, and commanded the doorkeeper to watch. Watch therefore, for you do not know when the master of the house is coming—in the evening, at midnight, at the crowing of the rooster, or in the morning—lest, coming suddenly, he find you sleeping. And what I say to you, I say to all: Watch!" (Mark 13:33–37)

This passage is similar to the one we've just looked at, with one important difference. St. Mark speaks of tasks that we have to perform: "each with his work."

What is your work? If you're standing in church during the Divine

Liturgy, you really only have one task: to worship God. I find the words of our Lord to be very comforting because they're so clear. But they also make me see that watchfulness/nepsis is not an option, it's a necessity: "What I say to you I say to all: Watch."

Chapter Ten

Two Kinds of Prayer

Now we're starting to get serious about attacking boredom in church. Nepsis. Guarding the mind and heart—these are difficult assignments, but well worth the effort. If you decide to undertake this effort, you should tell your spiritual father so he can offer direction and support.

Look at this quotation from St. Seraphim of Sarov:

> When the mind and heart are united in prayer and the thoughts of the soul are not distracted, the heart is kindled with a spiritual warmth out of which shines the light of Christ filling all the inner man with peace and joy. But if during prayer your mind is captured and your thoughts despoiled, then you must humble yourself before the Lord God and ask forgiveness, saying: *I have sinned, O Lord, in word, deed, thought and with all my senses.*[16]

When it comes to the question of watchfulness, St. Seraphim speaks specifically to prayer. It's the kind of praying you're doing in the Divine Liturgy that determines the quality of the time you spend there.

St. Seraphim speaks about two parts of us that participate in prayer: the mind and the heart. It's like when you're cooking an egg—you have to have

---

16 Archimandrite Lazarus (Moore), *An Extraordinary Peace: St. Seraphim, Flame of Sarov* (Port Townsend, WA: Anaphora Press, 2009), p. 153.

a pan and a spatula. You've got a pan but no spatula? No egg for you. Spatula but no pan? No egg for you, either. You've got to have both.

The Mind

Here's what it really comes down to: Where is your mind when your body's in church?

When we desire to guard our thoughts, eyes, and mouth in order to enter completely into the worship of God, it is extremely important that we do this by fixing our minds *on God*. There are non-Christian religions that try to "empty" the mind and heart as a spiritual discipline. This is not nepsis. Their goal is to create a completely vacant space inside your heart/mind. On the other hand, there are many people—people who fill churches every Sunday—who allow their minds to wander everywhere *except* toward God. They certainly have something on their minds, but it's not God.

Our goal as Orthodox Christians must be to free the mind from earthly distractions so we can give ourselves completely to God. We sing about this during the Divine Liturgy: "Let us who mystically portray the cherubim, and sing the thrice-holy hymn to the life-giving Trinity, now lay aside every care of life, that we may receive the King of all." See what that says? Lay aside the cares of life and receive the King. That's what nepsis is: laying aside the cares of this life. School. Job. Car. Friends. The future. Lay it all aside for a little while and fill your mind with the King of all.

Do you see now why I say it's worth the effort? When someone says, "Church is boring," he's really saying, "When I come to church, I drag my problems along with me, like a dog trying to drag a dead deer around the yard." Why do that? Why not drop the problems off at the door and spend a few minutes each week living free of their weight?

Of course, most of us keep (mentally) going back outside during the

Divine Liturgy to rearrange, or reconsider, or just stare at our problems. But remember St. Seraphim's advice: When your mind wanders, you should humble yourself and call out to God, "I have sinned, O Lord, in word, deed, thought and with all my senses." Repent that you allowed your mind to wander, and bring it back into the church.

The Heart

But listen to this: If the mind is the dog out in the yard chewing on a dead deer, the heart is the dog's owner standing in the doorway. The owner calls out to the dog to leave the deer alone and come inside, and the dog does what? Some dogs obey immediately and come to the owner, while other dogs don't feel as much like listening. The second kind spends a little more time in the yard messing around with the deer. Then a battle starts: the owner yells for the dog, and the dog tries to figure out how he can enjoy both things: the rotting deer and the owner's pleasure.

The key is to train the dog—in other words, to allow your *heart* to train your *mind* to pray. You know your heart draws you toward the church. You can sense God is there, love is there. Acceptance, forgiveness, peace. (Certainly, the church also has people in it, and sometimes people are not accepting or forgiving or peaceful. Don't think about that. Right now, keep your attention on God.)

Many times I have met people who haven't been to church in a long time, and they say to me, "I really need to get back to church." Why do they say that? To make the priest feel good? No! They say it almost in spite of themselves. They say it even though their habit for years has been to do something else on Sunday mornings. They say it because they have heard their hearts saying to them, every Sunday and every feast day, "You need to be in church."

The heart knows God, or at least part of it does. We can try to give our hearts to silly and useless things, but we can never completely overcome that one small part of it, the voice of the heart that never stops talking about God. Some people spend their whole lives filling their hearts with noise in order to drown out that voice. And usually it works. But the voice itself never stops.

And what is the conduit for the person who wants to drown out the divine voice in his heart? The mind. The mind carries us to the places where we can find noise. Old songs, plans for revenge, perverse fantasies, worries, self-loathing, and a thousand TV programs and movies—that basically sums up the mind.

The only hope is to reverse the flow. Let the heart teach the mind a few things, rather than the other way around. The heart of the Christian knows what is good and what is bad—listen to it. You force the mind to listen to the heart, like putting the dog on a leash. Then you tell it to go where you want it to go.

St. Paul talks to us about joining the two parts together in order to pray fruitfully: "What is *the conclusion* then? I will pray with the spirit, and I will also pray with the understanding. I will sing with the spirit, and I will also sing with the understanding" (1 Cor. 14:15). St. Paul is speaking about praying in a heavenly language, and he makes this point: If you pray in a language you don't understand, your heart prays, but your mind doesn't. You ought to pray in a language you understand, thereby giving your heart the necessary control over the mind. They can cooperate, and that makes your prayer real.

Here's another way of looking at it: The part of the Liturgy that begins, "I believe in one God, the Father Almighty, maker of heaven and earth" is called the "Creed." But its original name is the "Symbol of Faith." I like that name better, because when we say the Creed, we declare the rational particulars of our faith. We talk about the existence of God, the coming of Christ, the Resurrection, the Holy Spirit, and so on. These words speak to the mind; they teach us and remind us about our faith. *But these words are not our faith.* Our faith is in our minds *and* our hearts. Our faith is not something we say, but something we are. Of course, we cannot have faith in our hearts without knowing what we believe in—and so the Creed is extremely important. But the words of the Creed are only a symbol of what is in our hearts.

Finally, let me quote St. Simeon the New Theologian on the heart's ability to cure the mind:

> When the devil with his demons had succeeded in having man banished from the garden of Eden through transgression, and in separating him from God, he acquired access to the reasoning power of every man, so that he can agitate a man's mind by day or by night; sometimes much, sometimes a little, and sometimes exceedingly. And there is no protection against this except through constant remembrance of God; in other words, if the memory of God, engraved in the heart by the power of the cross, strengthens the mind in its steadfastness.[17]

And what other name do we give to the constant remembrance of God? Nepsis.

This is an extremely important point, and I'll use it to lead us from the two parts of us that pray to the two different kinds of prayer. We've spoken of the two elements of prayer: the mind and the heart. I like to link these two elements to the two kinds of prayer, public and private. Public prayer feeds the mind, and private prayer feeds the heart. Remember what I said before? You need both.

---

17   *Writings from the Philokalia, op cit.,* pp. 30–31.

Public Prayer

By *public prayer* I mean the prayer you do in church: Vespers, Orthros, sacraments, the Divine Liturgy, and all the other services of the church. During public prayer, you are not the one saying the words, at least most of the time. A chanter is saying them, or the priest or deacon, or someone is reading from the Scripture. Public prayer is the focus of this book—how to make public prayer meaningful, even though it might seem like you're just sitting or standing there.

I have had people tell me they find it much easier to pray without distractions, so they decide to pray only at home. They want to skip public prayer altogether and pray only privately, like the folks who watch the Divine Liturgy on TV. No. You need to be in church. You need to learn things about *what* you believe in order to know *how* to believe.

Look at it this way. All of us, at a certain age, began to get excited about getting a driver's license. The driver's license in our society represents a rite of passage, an assumption of responsibility, and the promise of freedom. It is an exciting time. I can still remember that first time I drove alone. I went to get a gallon of milk at a store that I had walked to or ridden my bike to a thousand times. But—you know what I mean—that time was different. As soon as I got back home, I asked my mother if she needed anything else.

It's a great feeling to learn to drive, but you can't only enjoy the *feelings* associated with driving; you actually have to *know how* to drive. If you get into the car and yell, "Engine, begin!"—no driving for you. If you start the engine and drive through your neighbor's lawn—no driving for you, either. If you drive through red lights or don't obey other traffic rules, the good feelings you associate with driving will soon evaporate under a mountain of fines and tubby insurance bills.

Same with prayer. You need to know how to pray just as much as you need to know how to drive. There are many people who don't know how to pray, and they do the equivalent of never starting the engine or driving through people's lawns. They don't get it right, and so even though they might have the good feelings associated with praying, those good feelings soon evaporate because the know-how of prayer is missing.

And where can you learn to pray? The church. Nowhere else. That's where public prayer takes place, prayer that not only brings you *to* God, but also teaches you *about* God.

I'll give you an example from Scripture—let's look at our Lord while He prays. In John 11:41–42, Jesus raised Lazarus from the dead. The people took Him to the tomb where they had placed Lazarus's body. He told them to take the stone away:

> Then they took away the stone *from the place* where the dead man was lying. And Jesus lifted up *His* eyes and said, "Father, I thank You that You have heard Me. And I know that You always hear Me, but because of the people who are standing by I said *this*, that they may believe that You sent Me."

Is that a prayer? Is it a prayer when you don't really need to say it, but you say it so the people around you can hear and learn something? Yes! The church does that all the time. When our Lord prayed at that moment, outside the tomb of Lazarus, He prayed in order to feed the minds of the people standing around. "Because of the people who are standing by." Those people were on our Lord's mind. He wanted them to know about prayer, about Himself, about the resurrecting power of God.

This is the most public of public prayers. Think of this prayer from the Divine Liturgy:

It is proper and it is right to hymn You, to bless You, to praise You, to thank You, to worship You in every place of Your dominion. For You are God inexpressible, inconceivable, invisible, incomprehensible, eternally existing, eternally the same, You and Your only-begotten Son and Your Holy Spirit.

We call these the Anaphora Prayers (the translation might be a little different in your parish). But listen. Does God need to be reminded that He is inexpressible? Or eternally the same? Obviously not. God does not need to be reminded of anything—we do! While you are praying any of the words of the Liturgy—and always remember, the words of the Liturgy are indeed prayers—allow them to teach you about the faith. Allow them to fill you with the One we pray to and teach you why we pray. Allow them to teach you what we believe.

This is why you need to participate in public prayer. This is why you need to pay attention during public prayer and avoid bovining. Please don't think this book is about teaching you to pray the Jesus Prayer in church so you don't get bored. It's not. You need to pray the prayers *of* the church *with* the church *in* the church in order to learn from them about the character and being of God. Without this public prayer instruction, your prayers will become self-directed and deluded.

Private Prayer

By *private prayer* I mean the prayer you do outside the Divine Liturgy, the prayer you pray by yourself. That might consist of memorized prayers you say each day, perhaps before an icon in your room. Or it might consist of times when you speak to God in your own words. Both of these are important. Sometimes we even pray private prayers in the church, like when you pray intercessory prayers for the people standing around you.

But there is another way to pray private prayers, and that is the Jesus Prayer, the prayer of the heart: "Lord Jesus Christ, Son of God, have mercy on me, a sinner." You know about this prayer. It's the breath of every good monastic. This prayer is for always, not only when you're outside the church, but in church as well. After all, you don't stop breathing when you enter a church.

I myself am a novice and a dilettante when it comes to the prayer of the heart. I have stood in the doorway looking into the mansion, but have not gone in, and so I can only urge you to stand with me. Perhaps you will have a better faith than mine and enter. We all must try, because all the effort we make to follow the commandments of God, all the effort we make to bring ourselves to true worship of Him falls short unless we have fixed the prayer in our hearts:

> On your path of obedience to the commandments seek the Lord in your heart. When you listen to John, crying in the wilderness, "Prepare ye the way of the Lord, make his paths straight" (Mark i.3), understand by these words commandments for the hearts as well as for actions; for it is impossible rightly to follow the commandments and to do rightly unless the heart too is right.[18]

When we pray the prayer of the heart, time does not matter. Time matters when we pray publically, but time does not matter when we pray the prayer of the heart. Can you imagine being bored when praying the prayer of the heart? Certainly not. If you were, you would just stop—that's the "private" of private prayer. But give it time. You'll find that the passage

---

18 *Writings from the Philokalia, op. cit.*, p. 40.

of time stops, boredom stops, everything stops when you fix the prayer in your heart.

You've seen people with prayer ropes wrapped around their wrists; perhaps you have one yourself. The idea is that you pray one repetition of the Jesus Prayer for every knot. Some prayer ropes have beads on them. When you reach a bead you're supposed to pray the Lord's Prayer, the "Our Father." What peace fills your heart! Just compare the feeling of praying the Lord's Prayer with a group of people before a meal, versus praying it alone after you've prayed twenty-five Jesus Prayers. Or fifty, or a hundred. The Jesus Prayer ushers into your body and soul such a wealth of joy and calm.

Practice. Nothing good comes without practice. Prayer is the good thing you can carry with you everywhere—it's the portal that opens the way to God.

Abba John Kolob used to say, "I am like a man who is sitting under a great tree, and sees multitudes of wild beasts and creeping things coming towards him. Because he is unable to stand up against them, he runs, goes up the tree, and is delivered. In this manner I sit in my cell, I see evil thoughts coming against me, and because I cannot stand against them I flee and take refuge in God by prayer. I am delivered from the enemies, and I live forever."[19]

---

19   E. A. Wallis Budge, trans., *The Paradise of the Holy Fathers*, vol. 2 (Putty, NSW, Australia: St. Shenouda Coptic Orthodox Monastery, 2008), p. 221.

Chapter Eleven

The One Thing You Need

SOMETIMES I WISH I could find that one perfect tool that would help me to focus my mind on God. But what would that be? A new icon, a prayer rope, the latest book—these things capture my attention for a short period of time, but then my mind wants something else, something newer. That's probably why my mind doesn't like church, because large parts of it consist of the same thing over and over. My mind craves new things all the time to feed its restlessness.

I recently needed to fly a long distance. The airline I flew on had screens on the back of every seat, and the flight attendants passed out headphones at the beginning of the flight. The device at each seat had an amazing array of amusements: games, travel videos, TV shows, movies, music videos, and a bunch of other choices. I had my own remote, so I could choose exactly what I wanted to watch on my own little entertainment center. I played with it for a little while when we first took off, then decided I would spend some time praying and just enjoying the fact that I had nothing at all to do. Silence. That's what I wanted, a little silence.

This is the one thing we need more than anything. More than food, more than sleep, more than bathrooms, we need silence. We need it more than anything because we don't get it, and lack of silence starves our souls. We need it more than anything else because our world rages against it and our sinful minds join in. Soon we find ourselves not only surrounded by noise, but also with a perverse desire for more and more noise.

We love silence for a little while, but then it gets boring. As I sat on that plane, with the headphones on the seat next to me, the screen in front of me, and the remote in my hand, my mind started complaining. Sure, I had my prayer rope, and I wanted silence. *But hey*, my mind said to me, *we're going to be sitting in this seat for eleven hours. Why don't we start with a good movie, then I'll let you have all the silence you want.* Okay, I thought. I'll just watch a movie, then pray.

Eleven hours later we were getting off the plane. I had watched three movies, a dozen or so TV programs, a travel video, and, as we began our descent, I spent probably a half hour staring at a nifty little feature where passengers could see what the pilots could see via a camera on the tip of the plane. What about prayer? What about silence?

Silence is a medicine our minds do not like to take. Silence is an exercise our minds like to avoid, "just for today." Silence frees us from the weight of the world, but our minds like the weight of the world. Our minds get frightened and bored easily.

The first time I put my dog in a car, when he was a puppy, he was so nervous he threw up. I told him we were in the car in order to go to the best dog-walking place in the entire universe, but he couldn't hear me. He tried to keep his eyes away from the windows so he would not see the world flying by faster than he could imagine. He was shivering all over as if he were freezing, even though it was a hot day.

Today, he launches into a frenzy of barking and spinning in little circles when he hears the word *car*. He loves the car. It takes him places he wants to go (usually). So it is with silence. When you first try it, your mind starts pacing like a coke addict on his first day in rehab. It yells, *I don't like this!* a hundred times. It rapidly starts suggesting other things you could be doing. But when you embrace silence and learn to use it as a tool that (spiritually) takes you places you want to go, you start to look forward to it and long for it when you're not getting enough.

Our model for the love of silence is Mary, the Mother of our Lord. Let's look at some of the places where she speaks in the Gospels and learn from her the inestimable value of silence.

The Annunciation: Mary Says "Yes" to God

We'll start with the Annunciation, where we can see the way the Theotokos used silence as her weapon against the powers of darkness.

What is different about the appearance of the Archangel Gabriel to Zacharias at the beginning of the first chapter of Luke and the same angel's appearance to the Theotokos just after that? Fear. This is the appearance to Zacharias: "Then an angel of the Lord appeared to him, standing on the right side of the altar of incense. And when Zacharias saw *him*, he was troubled, and fear fell upon him" (Luke 1:11–12).

And to Mary:

Now in the sixth month the angel Gabriel was sent by God to a city of Galilee named Nazareth, to a virgin betrothed to a man whose name was Joseph, of the house of David. The virgin's name *was* Mary. And having come in, the angel said to her, "Rejoice, highly favored one, the Lord *is* with you; blessed *are* you among women!" But when she saw *him*, she was troubled at his saying, and considered what manner of greeting this was. (vv. 26–29)

Both Zacharias and Mary are "troubled" at the sight of the angel, which makes sense. Everyone in Scripture who encounters an angel (when they realize it is indeed an angel) is shaken by the experience. I've never seen an angel, but I can gather from reading Scripture that their appearance is very different from the way it's portrayed in popular culture, with a white robe and wings made from gauze and so on. Angels are serious beings, and they serve God. There would be something wrong with you if you were not troubled when you saw one.

But both Zacharias and Mary felt something else quickly upon the heels of their agitation. Zacharias was afraid, while Mary was thoughtful. When I read about Zacharias, again, I understand his reaction. I try to imagine what it would be like to have an angel appear before me. Would an angel sent by God know everything about me? Would he have insight into my interior life, my secrets and my thoughts? If that's the case, then I can just imagine what expression would be on the angel's face as he looked at me. Disappointment, anger, disgust—these are the first words that come to mind. I would be wise to be afraid, as Zacharias was.

In that context, think for a moment about Mary's reaction to the angel. She, like Zacharias, understood that the angel knew everything about her. Her lack of fear rings forth through the words of Scripture with the sound of her humility, her guilelessness, her purity. She had longed her whole life for nothing except God. So for the angel to read her thoughts and intentions would be for him to see a wholehearted desire to know and submit to the thoughts of God, a single purpose toward holiness. She was not afraid because she had nothing to fear. The angel had greeted her with a greeting she had never heard before, with a divine blessing, and so she wondered what that blessing could mean. This, again, is understandable, but only if the person considering the angel's greeting is wholly and completely devoted to God.

In both cases, Zacharias and Mary, the angel then explains his appearing. He has come to announce the births of two children, both of whom will serve the eternal purposes of God. In both cases the parents-to-be ask for clarification—but look how differently the angel reacts to their requests. This is what the Scripture tells us about Zacharias:

> And Zacharias said to the angel, "How shall I know this? For I am an old man, and my wife is well advanced in years." And the angel answered and said to him, "I am Gabriel, who stands in the presence of God, and was sent to speak to you and bring you these glad tidings. But behold, you will be mute and not able to speak until the day these things take place, because you did not believe my words which will be fulfilled in their own time."(Luke 1:18–20)

Now look at the story of Mary:

> Then Mary said to the angel, "How can this be, since I do not know a man?" And the angel answered and said to her, "*The* Holy Spirit will come upon you, and the power of the Highest will overshadow you; therefore, also, that Holy One who is to be born will be called the Son of God. Now indeed, Elizabeth your relative has also conceived a son in her old age; and this is now the sixth month for her who was called barren. For with God nothing will be impossible." (vv. 34–37)

Zacharias asks for clarification, and the angel gets angry with him and takes away his ability to speak. That's a problem for a priest. On the other hand, the Theotokos asks for clarification, and the angel gladly complies. He does not get angry. Notice that Gabriel tells Mary about Elizabeth's pregnancy. I can almost hear him adding the words, "Oh, and if you go visit your cousin Elizabeth, and her husband can't greet you when you come in the door? That's all me."

So why the difference? Look at the last line of the story of Zacharias: "Because you did not believe my words." So I was right—angels can tell what we're thinking. Gabriel knew Zacharias did not believe him, perhaps was even laughing at the angel under his breath—*I don't know who you think you are, but you obviously haven't met my wife.* God had sent Gabriel to bring "good tidings," but Zacharias wouldn't listen. Gabriel's words, "I am Gabriel," do not suggest arrogance, but order. Zacharias had forgotten who was speaking to him. He had forgotten himself.

When Gabriel spoke to the Theotokos, he was aware of rank in that room as well. As we pray in many services, "More honorable than the cherubim and more glorious beyond compare than the seraphim, you who without stain gave birth to God the Logos, truly the Mother of God, you do we magnify." Mary had not yet ascended the throne, but she would—and Gabriel stood before her as a servant. When he visited Zacharias, he was speaking to a subordinate. When he visited Mary, he was speaking with a superior.

Mary's reaction becomes even more awesome when we consider the message itself. When the angel told Zacharias about Elizabeth's pregnancy, he described something that had occurred in Scripture several times already—to Sarah (Gen. 21:2), Rebecca (Gen. 25:21), Hannah (1 Sam. 1:7, 20), and the mother of Samson (Judg. 13:2–3)—a barren woman giving birth. But Zacharias doesn't believe him. Is this because he does not, deep down, believe the stories of the Scriptures? Perhaps this is why Gabriel gets so angry.

But when he appeared to the Theotokos, he described something that had *never* occurred in the history of the world and would never occur again—a virgin giving birth. But in this case, Mary believed—as soon as she made sure he knew she was a virgin. Zacharias did not believe the possible, but Mary believed the impossible. Why? "For with God, nothing will be impossible." Gabriel said this to her, but she knew it already.

She knew it already. Mary did not need to question Gabriel. She had come to believe in the awesome power of God long before the actual visit of the angel. Certainly, the visit needed to be made, because the Holy Spirit would not make a woman pregnant without her foreknowledge and consent. But in the silence of her heart, Mary had come to know God, His power and His will. At the Annunciation, she expressed authority, confidence, submission, and holiness—all, mostly, with her silence.

"My Soul Magnifies the Lord": Mary Sings about Her Place in History

Mary brought salvation into the world, and yet she says so few words in Scripture. She becomes, in her birthgiving, the new Eve, the new first mother of us all. Eve looked at things she should not have looked at, touched something she should not have touched, and ate something she should not have eaten. But her sin was compounded by her words: "The serpent deceived me, and I ate" (Gen. 3:13). Her desire was to use words to blame someone else for her sin—just like all of us often do.

Mary was very different than that. One passage in the New Testament stands out as the place where she used words—a place where she spoke longer than anywhere else—the Magnificat. Like the old Eve of Genesis, the new Eve also points to someone else with her words. But whereas the old Eve points to the devil, blaming him for her sin, the new Eve points to God, praising Him for His love of mankind:

And Mary said:

"My soul magnifies the Lord,

And my spirit has rejoiced in God my Savior.

For He has regarded the lowly state of His maidservant;

For behold, henceforth all generations will call me blessed.

For He who is mighty has done great things for me,

And holy *is* His name.

And His mercy *is* on those who fear Him

From generation to generation.

He has shown strength with His arm;

He has scattered *the* proud in the imagination of their hearts.

He has put down the mighty from *their* thrones,

And exalted *the* lowly.

He has filled *the* hungry with good things,

And *the* rich He has sent away empty.

He has helped His servant Israel,

In remembrance of *His* mercy,

As He spoke to our fathers,

To Abraham and to his seed forever." (Luke 1:46–55)

Mary sings that her soul magnifies the Lord. She is wholly invested in bringing glory to God, such that the very center of her being praises God continually. Mary tells us something here—namely, that she has no interest in talking about herself. The appearance of the angel brings her one desire: she wants to rejoice in God.

She tells us that she considers herself of a "lowly state." Let's think about this for a moment. Do you know what we celebrate at the feast of the Entrance of the Theotokos into the Temple every November 21? Mary's parents, Joachim and Anna, took Mary to the temple in Jerusalem, where she was received by Zacharias the priest. He took her to the steps leading to the Holy of Holies, where only the high priest could go, and only once each year—and she *danced* into the Holy of Holies. Picture your priest on a Sunday morning taking a little girl from the parish, carrying her into the altar through the holy doors, putting her down in front of the altar, and then stepping back while she danced around the altar? I'll tell you the truth: it almost makes me faint to think about it. And yet that was what happened with Mary, and the Holy Spirit was so strong in her that she stayed there for six years.

How, then, could she describe herself as being in a "lowly" state? One would expect her to say something like what St. Paul said when he described himself: "If anyone else thinks he may have confidence in the flesh, I more so: circumcised the eighth day, of the stock of Israel, *of* the tribe of Benjamin, a Hebrew of the Hebrews; concerning the law, a Pharisee; concerning zeal, persecuting the church; concerning the righteousness which is in the law, blameless" (Phil. 3:4–6). St. Paul had every right to remind us of his outstanding upbringing, training, and character. But how many times did he *dance* in the Holy of Holies? Zero.

Here's my point: The Theotokos was telling the truth when she said she saw herself as "lowly." This was not false modesty. And yet, applying the word *lowly* to her is difficult at best and perhaps impossible. How could she consider herself lowly when her childhood (which was barely over when she gave birth to Christ) was so . . . glorious? Miraculous? Unbelievable?

She considered herself lowly because of her closeness to God. The closer you get to God, the more you understand the extent of your lowliness. No matter what she would be used by God to accomplish on this earth, she would still understand her place before Him to be lowly.

Then she says all generations will call her blessed. The word *blessed* is important here. She did not say all generations would call her great, faithful, spiritual. We do! But that's not what she said. She said *blessed*. In her song of praise to God, she gives Him every bit of credit: "He . . . has done great things for me."

Mary is our mother. When we're born, we are the sons and daughters of Eve. But in Christ we become the sons and daughters of Mary.[20] Let's learn, then, from our mother how to use words only to glorify God. Learn how her words both express and nurture her humility. "The holy fathers teach that there are two kinds of humility: to regard oneself as lower than everyone else, and to ascribe all one's achievement to God. The first is the beginning, the second the consummation."[21]

There are two other times when Mary appears in the Gospel where she maintains complete silence. The first is in Luke 8:19–21:

Then His mother and brothers came to Him, and could not approach Him because of the crowd. And it was told Him *by some*, who said, "Your mother and Your brothers are standing outside, desiring to see You." But He answered and said to them, "My mother and My brothers are these who hear the word of God and do it."

Joseph had died, and his sons did not want to provide for Mary. They undoubtedly appealed to social customs of the time—namely, that it was up to her adult son, the only child she had, to provide for her. Some of them got together and took the Theotokos to where they knew Jesus was teaching, in order to "hand her over" to him. But when they arrived, the size of the crowd prevented them from getting close enough, so they boldly made themselves

---

20   I thank Fr. Chad Hatfield for this wonderful insight into the Theotokos.
21   *Writings from the Philokalia, op. cit.*, p. 238.

known: "We can't imagine why you religious fanatics want to listen to Jesus talking, but we have important business to conduct with him. Get out of the way!"

Two people there knew exactly what was happening: our Lord and His mother. Neither of them was agitated by the stepbrothers' plans. We can see the mother of God had been put in the position of an unwanted burden, like an elderly parent that gets shuffled from one reluctant child's house to another. But look at her face. When she saw the crowds that had come to hear her Son teach, she smiled. She would gladly sit in the corner of anyone's kitchen and get fed nothing but table scraps as long as she could know the words of the Archangel Gabriel were indeed true—she had borne the Savior of the world!

What a splendid picture of trust in God. How many times do I try to use my words to alert God to my situation—as if He doesn't know. "Uh, God, my car's in the shop right now and it's going to cost a lot to fix it . . ." Do I think of God as being super-busy today, so busy that He might have forgotten me? Look at the Theotokos; put yourself there by the Sea of Galilee and look at her smile. Joseph's sons rage around her, arguing with the crowd and demanding their rights, and she is at perfect peace.

Another time, Mary did indeed need someone to provide for her. Our Lord, from the cross, provided her with assistance:

> Now there stood by the cross of Jesus His mother, and His mother's sister, Mary the *wife* of Clopas, and Mary Magdalene. When Jesus therefore saw His mother, and the disciple whom He loved standing by, He said to His mother, "Woman, behold your son!" Then He said to the disciple, "Behold your mother!" And from that hour that disciple took her to his own *home*. (John 19:25–27)

The gruesome and maimed appearance of her Son filled the Theotokos with an indescribable sorrow. But this is what I want you to remember from this passage from the Scriptures: She never left. She stayed there—for Him, for St. John, for the women. She stayed for the soldiers. She stayed for you and for me. Perhaps every other mother, in that situation, would have had something to say. A song, like the Magnificat. A lament. A complaint. I want you to listen to her silence and feel her presence. No matter what you're doing or what you're going through, she's there. Just as she was at the cross of her Son.

Silence

Is church sometimes boring? And could it be that I'm actually offering silence as a solution? Yes to both. You and I are both citizens in a world that is under the control of the enemy. He knows your weakest point is your mind, and he will do whatever he can to win you to his side. His only weapon, since our Lord took suffering and death away from him, is distraction. Noise and toys. Can he really swing something shiny in front of your face and get you to forget the love and mercy of God? I don't know about you, but I'll admit that, yes, it works on me more often than I would like to admit.

What we've done here is to try to stop this from happening. This effort is the very foundation of the Christian life. But listen. We cannot live in the foundation of a house; we have to build on that foundation. Keep growing, keep moving upward. To quote again from *The Ascetical Homilies of St. Isaac the Syrian*: "Question: What bond restrains a man's mind from running after evil things? Answer: continually to search after wisdom, and to be insatiate for the doctrine of life; there is no stronger bond for the mind's unruliness than this."[22]

---

22   St. Isaac the Syrian, *op cit.*, p. 289.

I pray that you will "continually search after wisdom," and that this search will yield in you a great harvest of spiritual delight, noetic benefit, and communion with God.

Ancient Faith Publishing hopes you have enjoyed and benefited from this book. The proceeds from the sales of our books only partially cover the costs of operating our nonprofit ministry—which includes both the work of **Ancient Faith Publishing** (formerly known as Conciliar Press) and the work of **Ancient Faith Radio**. Your financial support makes it possible to continue this ministry both in print and online. Donations are tax-deductible and can be made at www.ancientfaith.com.

Bringing you Orthodox Christian music, readings, prayers,
teaching and podcasts 24 hours a day since 2004 at
www.ancientfaith.com

About the Author

Rev. Dr. David Smith is the pastor of St. Sophia's Greek Orthodox Church in Syracuse, New York. He and Presbytera Donna have four children.

Also by Fr. David Smith

Mary, Worthy of All Praise: Reflections on the Virgin Mary
The Paraklesis service offers the perfect vehicle for us to consider the place of Mary in our lives. Fr. David Smith shares with us his own personal meditations on Mary, based upon his reflections on the Paraklesis service.

• Paperback, 118 pages (ISBN: 978-1-888212-71-6)
AFP Order No. 006599—$11.95*

Other Books of Interest

Let Us Attend
A Journey
Through the Orthodox Divine Liturgy
by Father Lawrence Farley

Esteemed author and Scripture commentator Fr. Lawrence Farley provides a guide
to understanding the Divine Liturgy, and a vibrant reminder of the centrality of the
Eucharist in living the Christian life.

Every Sunday morning we are literally taken on a journey into the Kingdom of
God. Fr. Lawrence guides believers in a devotional and historical walk through the
Orthodox Liturgy. Examining the Liturgy section by section, he provides both historical
explanations of how the Liturgy evolved and devotional insights aimed at helping us
pray the Liturgy in the way the Fathers intended. In better understanding the depth of
the Liturgy's meaning and purpose, we can pray it properly. If you would like a deeper
understanding of your Sunday morning experience so that you can draw closer to God,
then this book is for you.

> • Paperback, 104 pages (ISBN: 978-1-888212-87-7)
> **AFP Order No. 007295—$10.95***

Traveling Companions
Walking with the Saints of the Church
by Christopher Moorey

Do you long to establish a relationship with the saints, but find them—or the
volumes written about them—a little intimidating? The saints started out as
ordinary Christians, just like us, and they are waiting to accompany us on our
journey to heaven if we will only reach out our hands. *Traveling Companions*
is a manageable volume that briefly introduces saints from a variety of times,
places, and walks of life, all in language that brings them close to contemporary
readers' lives. You're sure to find companions here that you will be happy to
walk with all the way to the Kingdom.

> • Paperback, 296 pages (ISBN: 978-1-936270-47-7)
> **AFP Order No. 008284—$18.95***

The Scent of Holiness
Lessons from a Women's Monastery
by Constantina Palmer
Every monastery exudes the scent of holiness, but women's monasteries have their own special flavor. Join Constantina Palmer as she makes frequent pilgrimages to a women's monastery in Greece and absorbs the nuns' particular approach to their spiritual life. If you're a woman who's read of Mount Athos and longed to partake of its grace-filled atmosphere, this book is for you. Men will find it a fascinating read as well.
  • Paperback, 288 pages (ISBN: 978-1-936270-42-2)
    AFP Order No. 008272—$18.95*

Words for Our Time
The Spiritual Words of Matthew the Poor
The twentieth-century elder Abba Matta of Egypt, known in the West as Matthew the Poor, is widely regarded as the greatest Egyptian elder since St. Antony the Great. He produced a huge and varied body of work in Arabic, only a little of which has been translated into English. In addition, a great many of his informal talks to monks and visitors were recorded. This volume is the first appearance in English of a small selection of these talks.

Abba Matta had a marvelous ability to communicate the deepest spiritual truths in the simplest and most practical language, making them accessible to laypeople as well as monastics. He speaks to the heart rather than the head, gently exhorting the reader to pursue a deeper life in Christ. To read these talks is to sit at the feet of one of the greatest spiritual teachers of our age.
  • Paperback, 208 pages (ISBN: 978-1-936270-45-3)
    AFP Order No. 008282—$16.95*

A Patristic Treasury
Early Church Wisdom for Today's Christians
James R. Payton, Jr. (editor)
The writings of the Church Fathers are regularly lauded but rarely read, partly because their sheer volume is so daunting. Yet they constitute the "first storey" of the Christian faith, built upon its apostolic foundation, which we ignore at our peril. Patristic scholar James Payton has made the Fathers easily accessible by selecting passages that are devotionally stimulating, doctrinally thought-provoking, or epigrammatically striking. With his help, the average Christian can find stimulation, comfort, challenge, and inspiration in the Church Fathers.
  • Paperback, 480 pages (ISBN: 978-1-936270-44-6)
    AFP Order No. 008281—$29.95*

*Prices do not include applicable sales tax or shipping and handling.

Prices were current on August 1, 2013, and are subject to change.

To request a catalog, to obtain complete ordering information, or to place a credit card order, please call us at (800) 967-7377 or (219) 728-2216 or log onto our website: www.store.ancientfaith.com.